Gabriel Gaté

100 best cakes
& desserts

Gabriel Gaté

100 best cakes & desserts

SBS

hardie grant books
MELBOURNE · LONDON

contents

Baked Lemon Cheesecake

SERVES 12

People of all ages love this light baked cheesecake. Bake it at least 4 hours before serving, and store it in the fridge if you plan to serve it much later than that.

180 g (6 oz) plain sweet biscuits (cookies)
125 g (4 oz) butter, melted
40 g (1½ oz/¼ cup) raw almonds, very finely chopped
400 ml (13 fl oz) milk
60 g (2 oz) unsalted butter
60 g (2 oz/½ cup) cornflour (cornstarch)
2 egg yolks
350 g (12 oz) cream cheese
juice of 2 lemons
5 egg whites
pinch of cream of tartar
145 g (5 oz/⅔ cup) caster (superfine) sugar
icing (confectioners') sugar, for dusting

Preheat the oven to 150°C (300°F). Butter a 24 cm (9½ in) springform cake tin.

Place the biscuits in a food processor and process until they have the consistency of raw sugar. Using a wooden spoon, combine the biscuit crumbs, melted butter and chopped almonds. Press the crumb mixture into the prepared tin, covering two-thirds of the side of the tin. Refrigerate while preparing the filling.

Place 350 ml (12 fl oz) of the milk and the unsalted butter in a saucepan and bring to the boil. Combine the cornflour, egg yolks and remaining milk in a bowl. Mix into the hot milk mixture and cook over low heat, stirring occasionally, for 5 minutes. Remove from the heat, stir in the cream cheese, add the lemon juice and mix until smooth.

Using electric beaters, beat the egg whites and cream of tartar until stiff peaks form. Gradually add the sugar and beat until the egg whites are firm. Gently fold the beaten egg whites into the cream cheese mixture.

Pour the filling onto the chilled crumb mixture, smooth the top and bake for 1 hour 20 minutes or until the centre is set. Set aside to cool completely, then remove from the tin and refrigerate.

Remove the cheesecake from the refrigerator 20 minutes before serving. Serve dusted with a little icing sugar.

Apricot and Hazelnut Dacquoise

SERVES 10

For this recipe you can prepare the meringues and the apricot purée a day ahead, and assemble the dacquoise just before serving.

60 g (2 oz/½ cup) ground hazelnuts, toasted
1 tablespoon cornflour (cornstarch)
180 g (6 oz) caster (superfine) sugar
4 large egg whites
pinch of cream of tartar
¼ teaspoon vinegar
¼ teaspoon pure vanilla extract
80 g (3 oz) dried apricots
375 ml (13 fl oz/1½ cups) cream, whipped
    until firm
20 roasted hazelnuts, chopped
90 g (3 oz/1 cup) flaked almonds, toasted
icing (confectioners') sugar, for dusting

Preheat the oven to 180°C (350°F). Draw a 20 cm (8 in) circle on three sheets of baking paper and use them to line three baking trays.

Combine the toasted ground hazelnuts, cornflour and one-quarter of the sugar.

Using electric beaters, beat the egg whites and cream of tartar on medium to high speed until almost stiff. Reduce speed to low, gradually add the remaining sugar, then the vinegar and vanilla extract, and beat until stiff peaks form.

Fold the ground hazelnut mixture into the beaten whites. Spoon the mixture into a piping bag fitted with a 1 cm (½ in) plain nozzle. Pipe three discs inside the circles on the baking paper, starting from the outside and moving inwards to fill the inside of the discs. Bake the discs for 25–30 minutes or until the meringue is firm and dry. Set aside to cool.

Place the dried apricots in a saucepan and cover with cold water. Bring to the boil, then cook for 10 minutes. Drain the apricots and blend to a fine purée. Set aside to cool.

Spread two meringue discs with apricot purée, then top with two-thirds of the whipped cream and sprinkle with the chopped hazelnuts. Stack the meringue discs, placing the plain one on top. Spread the remaining cream over the side of the dacquoise and lightly press on the flaked almonds. Dust the top with icing sugar and serve.

Orange and Almond Cake

SERVES 8–10

Make this flourless cake in the winter months when oranges are at their best. The first step is quite unusual as you need to simmer two whole oranges in water for 2 hours. After that, it's a piece of cake!

2 unblemished oranges
235 g (8½ oz/1½ cups) blanched almonds
230 g (8 oz/1 cup) caster (superfine) sugar
5 large eggs
1 teaspoon baking powder
icing (confectioners') sugar, for dusting

Wash the oranges and place in a saucepan. Cover with cold water and bring to the boil, then cover the pan and simmer for 2 hours. Top up the water during cooking when necessary. Drain the oranges and set aside to cool.

Preheat the oven to 180°C (350°F). Butter a 20 cm (8 in) round cake tin.

Place the almonds and sugar in a food processor and blend until the almonds are in quite small pieces. Some of them will be finely ground. Transfer to a plate.

Place the whole oranges in the food processor and blend to a purée. Add the almond mixture and briefly blend before adding in the eggs and baking powder and blending until smooth.

Pour the mixture into the prepared tin and bake for 1 hour or until a bamboo skewer inserted into the middle comes out dry. Set aside for 10 minutes before turning out onto a wire rack.

Serve the cake dusted with icing sugar.

Black Forest Roulade

SERVES 8–10

It's so much fun to make a roulade. I'm always amazed at how popular this Black Forest version is. Make sure you use good-quality chocolate.

CHOCOLATE SPONGE
2 tablespoons Dutch (unsweetened) cocoa powder
80 g (3 oz) plain (all-purpose) flour
4 large eggs
100 g (3½ oz) caster (superfine) sugar
50 g (2 oz) butter, just melted

2 tablespoons Kirsch or brandy
500 ml (17 fl oz/2 cups) cream, whipped until firm
280 g (10 oz) drained Morello cherries
100 g (3½ oz) dark chocolate
icing (confectioners') sugar, for dusting
Crème Anglaise (page 185), to serve (optional)

To make the chocolate sponge, preheat the oven to 180°C (350°F). Butter a 36 x 26 cm (14 x 10 in) Swiss roll (jelly roll) tin and line it with baking paper. Butter and flour the baking paper.

Sift the cocoa and flour together.

Using electric beaters, beat the eggs and sugar until the mixture forms a thick ribbon. Fold in the sifted flour and cocoa until just combined. Gently but quickly incorporate the melted butter. Pour the mixture into the prepared tin and spread to the edges. Bake for 8 minutes or until firm to the touch.

Turn the warm chocolate sponge out onto a clean tea towel. Peel off the paper and roll up the sponge by lifting the tea towel. Set aside to cool.

Unroll the chocolate sponge and sprinkle with the Kirsch. Spread a little over half of the whipped cream over the chocolate sponge. Arrange the cherries on top of the cream. Carefully roll up the sponge so that it is firm but not too tight.

Using a spatula, spread the remaining cream over the roll. Grate the chocolate over the cake and refrigerate for at least 1 hour. Lightly dust with icing sugar just before slicing and serve with the crème anglaise, if using.

Pavlova with Exotic Fruits

SERVES 8–10

When cooking a pavlova, the oven temperature must not be too high or too low. The meringue should end up crunchy on the outside without being too browned. You may need to experiment to work out the right temperature for your oven, as each oven is different.

4 egg whites

pinch of cream of tartar

230 g (8 oz/1 cup) caster (superfine) sugar

1 teaspoon cornflour (cornstarch)

1 teaspoon vinegar

1 teaspoon pure vanilla extract

375 ml (13 fl oz/1½ cups) cream, whipped until firm

selection of seasonal fruits, such as strawberries, mango, pineapple, papaya, raspberries, bananas and cherries

pulp of 6 passionfruit

Preheat the oven to 220°C (430°F). Draw a 22 cm (8½ in) circle on a sheet of baking paper and place the paper on a baking tray, circle-side down.

Using electric beaters, beat the egg whites and cream of tartar until stiff peaks form. Gradually beat in the sugar until well incorporated. Using a rubber spatula, fold in the cornflour, vinegar and vanilla extract.

Heap the meringue mixture onto the prepared baking tray and spread out to fill the circle. Make the centre a little shallower than the side.

Reduce the oven to 120°C (250°F) and bake the meringue for 1½ hours. Remove from the oven and set aside to cool. The meringue may crack a little after cooking.

Spoon the whipped cream into the centre of the pavlova and top with pieces of fruit. Spoon the passionfruit pulp over the top and serve immediately.

Almond and Blueberry Galette

SERVES 8

A galette is the French term for a flat cake. I love the flavour of the cooked blueberries in this dish. You can also make eight small galettes using individual flan tins or muffin tins.

160 g (5½ oz) plain (all-purpose) flour, sifted
80 g (3 oz/¾ cup) ground almonds
200 g (7 oz) butter, cut into small cubes
2 teaspoons finely grated lemon zest
200 g (7 oz) caster (superfine) sugar
4 large egg yolks
50 g (2 oz) flaked almonds
200 g (7 oz) blueberries
cream, ice cream or a fruit sauce (pages 187 to 189), to serve

Place the flour and ground almonds in a bowl and make a well in the centre. Add the butter, lemon zest, sugar and 3½ egg yolks to the well. Using your fingertips, work these ingredients together first until just combined, then gradually incorporate the flour and ground almonds until a dough forms. Shape the dough into a ball, cover and refrigerate for 30 minutes.

Preheat the oven to 200°C (400°F). Butter a 24 cm (9½ in) flan tin and sprinkle the sides of the tin with the flaked almonds.

Cut the dough in half. Lightly flour the dough, your hands and the rolling pin and roll each dough half out to a circle to fit the tin. Place one round of dough in the tin. Top with the blueberries, leaving a 1 cm (½ in) border around the edge. Place the other round of dough on top. Mix the remaining ½ egg yolk with 1 teaspoon water and lightly brush over the top of the dough. Using a fork, mark a lattice pattern on top of the dough.

Bake the galette for 20 minutes, then reduce the oven to 180°C (350°F) and bake for a further 35 minutes or until the top is firm to the touch. Leave to cool before carefully turning out. Serve the galette with cream, ice cream or a fruit sauce (pages 187 to 189).

Almond and Blueberry Galette

Banana Loaf

MAKES 12 SLICES

I use olive oil instead of butter in this favourite family recipe, making it a good choice for those wanting to reduce their saturated fat intake. You can decorate the top of the loaf with thin slices of banana before baking.

115 g (4 oz/½ cup) caster (superfine) sugar

3 large eggs

2 teaspoons finely grated lemon zest

125 ml (4 fl oz/½ cup) mild-flavoured extra-virgin olive oil

150 g (5 oz/1 cup) wholemeal (whole-wheat) self-raising flour

55 g (2 oz/½ cup) ground almonds

1 teaspoon bicarbonate of soda (baking soda)

pinch of salt

155 g (5 oz/1 cup) finely grated carrot

2 bananas, mashed

60 g (2 oz/½ cup) sultanas (golden raisins)

12 pitted prunes

icing (confectioners') sugar, for dusting

250 ml (8½ fl oz/1 cup) cream, whipped until firm, to serve (optional)

Preheat the oven to 180°C (350°F). Butter a 25 x 11 cm (10 x 4½ in) loaf (bar) tin and line the base with baking paper.

Put the sugar, eggs and lemon zest in a large bowl and mix until thoroughly combined. Stir in the olive oil, flour, ground almonds, bicarbonate of soda and salt and mix until smooth. Stir in the grated carrot, mashed banana, sultanas and prunes.

Pour the mixture into the prepared tin and bake for about 1 hour or until a skewer inserted into the middle comes out clean. Set aside for about 10 minutes before turning out onto a wire rack to cool.

To serve, cut the loaf into slices and dust with icing sugar. Serve with a little whipped cream for a special treat.

Chocolate Profiteroles with Ice Cream

SERVES 6

I have a weakness for profiteroles. These little choux puffs can be filled with ice cream, custard or cream. I prefer ice cream, as I love the contrast between the hot chocolate sauce and the cold ice cream.

60 ml (2 fl oz/¼ cup) cream
200 g (7 oz/1⅓ cups) dark chocolate, chopped
1 quantity Choux Pastry, made into small
   choux puffs (page 178)
1 litre (34 fl oz/4 cups) Vanilla Ice Cream
   (page 128 or store-bought)

Bring the cream to the boil in a small saucepan. Stir in the chocolate over very low heat until it has melted. Keep the sauce warm.

Slice off the top of each choux puff and, using a teaspoon, fill with ice cream. Replace the lid on each choux puff and place in the freezer until they are ready to be served.

Just before serving, spoon the hot chocolate sauce over the profiteroles.

Strawberry Sponge Cake

SERVES 12–14

When our children were young they always asked us to make this cake and we all still love it. The strawberries can be replaced with other berries or soft fruits and you can use a custard instead of whipped cream.

250 g (9 oz) caster (superfine) sugar

8 large eggs

250 g (9 oz/1⅔ cups) plain (all-purpose) flour, sifted

100 g (3½ oz) butter, just melted

600 g (1 lb 5 oz) strawberries, hulled

155 g (5 oz/1¼ cups) icing (confectioners') sugar

200 ml (7 fl oz) cream, whipped until firm

Preheat the oven to 180°C (350°F). Butter and flour a 25 cm (10 in) round cake tin.

Using an electric mixer, beat the sugar and eggs for about 10 minutes or until the mixture forms a thick ribbon.

Add the sifted flour all at once and, using a rubber spatula, fold it into the egg mixture, gently but quickly. Mix in the melted butter, gently but quickly.

Pour the mixture into the prepared tin and smooth the top with a spatula. Bake for 30–40 minutes or until the cake is lightly browned and springs back when lightly touched in the centre. Set aside for a few minutes before gently turning out onto a wire rack to cool completely.

Mash two of the strawberries, then gradually stir in the icing sugar until the mixture has the consistency of icing (frosting).

Slice the remaining strawberries in half. Cut the sponge in half horizontally. Spread the bottom half with the whipped cream and top with two-thirds of the halved strawberries. Replace the top half of the cake and spread the icing over the top. Garnish with the remaining strawberry halves.

Butter Cake

SERVES 8–12

This cake, one of our family favourites when I was a boy, is one of the first cakes I learned to make. Its French name is *quatre quarts*, meaning 'four quarters', because the four main ingredients have the same weight.

180 g (6 oz) sugar
3 eggs
2 teaspoons finely grated lemon zest
180 g (6 oz) butter, just melted
180 g (6 oz) plain (all-purpose) flour

Preheat the oven to 180°C (350°F). Butter and flour a 23 cm (9 in) round cake tin or a 20 cm (8 in) square cake tin.

Using electric beaters, beat the sugar, eggs and lemon zest until creamy. Mix in the melted butter. Sift the flour over the top and fold in until just combined.

Pour the mixture into the prepared tin and bake for about 30 minutes or until a skewer inserted into the middle comes out clean. Set aside for about 10 minutes before turning out onto a wire rack to cool.

Pithiviers

SERVES 6–8

This classic French cake of almond cream in puff pastry is traditionally eaten on January 6th to celebrate Epiphany, the coming of the Magi.

125 g (4 oz) butter, softened
125 g (4 oz) caster (superfine) sugar
1 tablespoon finely grated orange zest
2 eggs plus 1 egg yolk, for brushing
125 g (4 oz/1¼ cups) ground almonds
1½ tablespoons rum
25 g (1 oz) plain (all-purpose) flour, sifted
500 g (1 lb 2 oz) Puff Pastry (page 180),
   or store-bought

Using electric beaters, beat the butter, sugar and orange zest until very pale. Beat in the two eggs one at a time, mixing well. Add the ground almonds and mix well. Add the rum and sifted flour and mix well. Spoon the almond cream into a piping bag without a nozzle.

Preheat the oven to 220°C (430°F). Line a baking tray with baking paper.

Cut the puff pastry in half and roll out to a 25 cm (10 in) square, about 5 mm (¼ in) thick. Cut out a 25 cm (10 in) circle from each square of pastry.

Place one of the pastry circles on the prepared tray. Using a small sharp knife, score an 18 cm (7 in) circle inside the pastry circle. Mix the egg yolk with 1 tablespoon water and brush around the outer edge of the pastry.

Pipe the almond cream into the centre circle, then cover with the second pastry circle and press the edges so the pastry sticks together. Brush the top with the remaining egg yolk. Using a small sharp knife, draw curved lines from the centre of the pastry to the edge to form a pattern.

Bake for 15 minutes, then reduce the oven to 200°C (400°F) and bake for a further 20–25 minutes or until the pastry is cooked and browned underneath.

Prune and Galliano Cake

SERVES 8–10

This cake looks really attractive when cooked in a kugelhopf tin, but you can also bake it in a ring (bundt) tin.

4 eggs

285 g (10 oz/1¼ cups) caster (superfine) sugar

310 ml (10 fl oz/1¼ cups) cream

2 tablespoons Galliano liqueur

300 g (10½ oz/2 cups) self-raising flour, sifted

2 tablespoons orange marmalade

30 g (1 oz/¼ cup) Dutch (unsweetened) cocoa powder, sifted

110 g (3½ oz/½ cup) pitted prunes, cut into small pieces

icing (confectioners') sugar or Dutch (unsweetened) cocoa powder, for dusting

Preheat the oven to 150°C (300°F). Butter and flour a 25 cm (10 in) kugelhopf tin or a 25 cm (10 in) ring (bundt) tin.

Using electric beaters, beat the eggs and sugar until thick and creamy. Fold in the cream and Galliano.

Lightly fold in the sifted flour. Spoon two-thirds of the mixture into the prepared tin.

Combine the marmalade, cocoa powder and chopped prunes, then mix into the remaining cake mixture. Pour this over the mixture in the tin, then lightly stir with the blade of a knife to obtain a slightly marbled effect.

Bake for 1–1¼ hours. Set aside to cool for 5 minutes before turning out onto a wire rack. Serve dusted with icing sugar or cocoa powder.

Lemon and Coconut Semolina Cake with Pistachios

SERVES 10

Once this cake is cooked, it's soaked with a lemon syrup. It's a beautiful cake that seems to please everyone. For me it's more an afternoon treat than a dessert.

125 g (4 oz) unsalted butter, softened
2 tablespoons finely grated lemon zest
230 g (8 oz/1 cup) caster (superfine) sugar
2 large eggs
90 g (3 oz/⅔ cup) pistachios, chopped
85 g (3 oz/⅔ cup) semolina
25 g (1 oz/¼ cup) desiccated (shredded) coconut
225 g (8 oz/1½ cups) self-raising flour, sifted
125 ml (4 fl oz/½ cup) milk
icing (confectioners') sugar, for dusting

LEMON SYRUP
115 g (4 oz/½ cup) caster (superfine) sugar
juice of 2 lemons

Preheat the oven to 200°C (400°F). Butter and flour a 25 cm (10 in) ring (bundt) tin.

Using electric beaters or a wooden spoon, beat the softened butter, lemon zest and sugar until light and fluffy. Beat in the eggs one at a time. Stir in two-thirds of the pistachios and all of the semolina, coconut, sifted flour and milk.

Pour the mixture into the prepared tin, smooth the top and bake for 10 minutes. Reduce the oven to 150°C (300°F) and cook for a further 30 minutes or until a skewer inserted into the middle comes out clean.

Meanwhile, to make the lemon syrup, combine the sugar, lemon juice and 125 ml (4 fl oz/½ cup) water in a small saucepan and boil for about 5 minutes. Set aside.

Leave the cooked cake in the tin for 5 minutes before pouring the syrup over the top. Set aside to cool completely before carefully turning out.

Sprinkle the cake with the remaining pistachios. Dust with icing sugar just before serving.

Confit Fruit Cake

MAKES 12–16 SLICES

This easy-to-make cake is perfect for a snack between meals with a cup of tea, coffee or hot chocolate. It keeps well for several days and is even better after one day.

60 g (2 oz/½ cup) sultanas (golden raisins) or raisins
1½ tablespoons rum, brandy or Grand Marnier
50 g (2 oz) glacé (candied) pears
50 g (2 oz) glacé (candied) apricots
6 each red and green glacé (candied) cherries
125 g (4 oz) butter, softened
125 g (4 oz) caster (superfine) sugar
1 tablespoon finely grated lemon zest
3 eggs
200 g (7 oz/1⅓ cups) self-raising flour, sifted
2 tablespoons apricot jam
2 tablespoons flaked almonds, toasted (optional)
icing (confectioners') sugar, for dusting (optional)

Combine the sultanas and rum in a bowl. Soak overnight or for at least 6 hours.

Preheat the oven to 200°C (400°F). Butter a 25 x 11 cm (10 x 4½ in) loaf (bar) tin.

Cut the glacé pears and apricots into cubes, about 8 mm (⅓ in) thick. Quarter the red and green glacé cherries.

Using electric beaters, beat the butter, sugar and lemon zest until light and creamy. Beat in the eggs one at a time. Add the sifted flour and mix until just combined.

Stir in the sultanas and rum and, using a wooden spoon, mix well by lifting the cake mixture rather than stirring it. Mix in the glacé pears, apricots and quartered cherries in the same way, but do not overmix.

Spoon the mixture into the prepared tin, smoothing the top a little. Bake for 10 minutes, then reduce the oven to 170°C (340°F) and bake for a further 45 minutes or until the top is firm to the touch. Set aside for 10 minutes before turning out onto a wire rack to cool completely.

Just before serving, brush the top of the cake with a little apricot jam, decorate with the toasted flaked almonds and dust with icing sugar, if using. Store the cake in a cake tin in a cool place.

Lemon and Coconut Semolina Cake with Pistachios

Confit Fruit Cake

Flourless Chocolate Cake with a Chocolate and Hazelnut Topping

SERVES 8–10

This is a superb version of a flourless chocolate cake. The crunch of the hazelnuts give it an extra dimension.

potato flour, for dusting
60 ml (2 fl oz/$\frac{1}{4}$ cup) cream
150 g (5 oz/1 cup) dark chocolate, chopped
4 large eggs, separated
100 g (3$\frac{1}{2}$ oz) caster (superfine) sugar
100 g (3$\frac{1}{2}$ oz/1 cup) ground almonds, toasted
60 g (2 oz/$\frac{1}{2}$ cup) sultanas (golden raisins)
1 tablespoon brandy
pinch of cream of tartar
6 glacé (candied) apricots, halved (optional)

ICING
2 tablespoons cream
100 g (3$\frac{1}{2}$ oz) dark chocolate, chopped
20 roasted hazelnuts, roughly chopped

Preheat the oven to 180°C (350°F). Butter a 25 cm (10 in) ring (bundt) tin, or a 22 cm (8$\frac{1}{2}$ in) round or square cake tin and dust with potato flour.

Bring the cream to the boil in a small saucepan. Remove from the heat and stir in the chocolate until melted.

Using electric beaters, beat the egg yolks and sugar until white and fluffy. Gently stir in the chocolate mixture, toasted ground almonds, sultanas and brandy.

Using electric beaters, beat the egg whites and cream of tartar until stiff peaks form. Fold the egg whites into the chocolate mixture.

Pour the mixture into the prepared tin and bake for 50 minutes or until the centre of the top is firm to the touch. Set aside for 15 minutes before carefully turning out onto a wire rack.

To make the icing (frosting), bring the cream to the boil in a small saucepan. Remove from the heat and stir in the chocolate until melted and smooth. Stir in the roasted hazelnuts. Pour the icing over the cake and decorate with the apricot halves, if using.

Caramel Paris Brest with Chocolate Hazelnut Cream

SERVES 10

Paris Brest is one of the most popular French patisseries. I love it.

170 g (6 oz/$^3/_4$ cup) caster (superfine) sugar
$^1/_2$ teaspoon red wine vinegar
1 quantity Choux Pastry, made into 10 Paris Brest (page 178)
80 g (3 oz) flaked almonds, toasted (optional)
80 g (3 oz) butter, softened
60 g (2 oz) chocolate hazelnut spread
1 quantity Crème Pâtissière (page 184)

Combine the sugar, vinegar and 60 ml (2 fl oz/$^1/_4$ cup) water in a small saucepan. Bring to the boil over medium heat, then cook until the mixture turns golden brown. Remove from the heat as the colour is changing to golden brown and very carefully dip the top of each Paris Brest ring into the caramel to lightly coat it. Place on a wire rack to cool. Sprinkle the flaked almonds on top of each Paris Brest, if using.

When the caramel is cold, split the rings in half horizontally.

Using electric beaters, beat the butter and chocolate hazelnut spread until well combined. Add the crème pâtissière and mix well.

Spoon the chocolate mixture into a piping bag fitted with a 1 cm ($^1/_2$ in) fluted nozzle. Pipe a ring of chocolate cream onto the pastry bases. Replace the tops and refrigerate until required.

Raspberry Choux Puffs

SERVES 10

I like to serve this popular dessert at the end of a Sunday family lunch. Plan ahead and cook the choux pastry and the crème pâtissière the day before you want to serve the dessert.

½ quantity Choux Pastry, made into 10 large choux puffs (page 178)
pulp of 2 passionfruit
1 quantity Crème Pâtissière (page 184)
250 ml (8½ fl oz/1 cup) cream, whipped until firm
600 g (1 lb 5 oz) raspberries
icing (confectioners') sugar, for dusting

Cut off the top of each choux puff to make a lid.

Whisk the passionfruit pulp with the crème pâtissière, then fold into the whipped cream. Spoon into a piping bag.

Place about eight raspberries in each choux puff. Pipe the custard over the raspberries, up to the rim of the choux puff, and top with more raspberries.

Replace the lid on each choux puff. Dust with icing sugar, garnish with a raspberry and serve immediately.

Apple Cake

SERVES 8–10

This is one of our family favourites and it's easy to make. I make it in a round cake tin. You can, of course, use a different-shaped tin. The cake keeps well for two to three days.

150 g (5 oz) butter, softened

145 g (5 oz/⅔ cup) caster (superfine) sugar, plus 1 tablespoon extra, for dusting

1 teaspoon finely grated lemon zest

3 eggs

150 g (5 oz/1 cup) white or wholemeal (whole-wheat) self-raising flour, sifted

30 g (1 oz/¼ cup) sultanas (golden raisins)

2 green apples

½ teaspoon ground cinnamon

70 g (2½ oz) smooth apricot jam, warmed

Preheat the oven to 200°C (400°F). Butter and flour a 20 cm (8 in) round cake tin.

Using electric beaters, beat the butter, sugar and lemon zest for a few minutes until light and creamy. Beat in the eggs, then fold in the sifted flour.

Carefully pour the mixture into the prepared tin. Tap the tin to evenly distribute the mixture and, if necessary, smooth the top with a spatula. Sprinkle the sultanas over the top.

Peel, core and halve the apples, then cut into 5 mm (¼ in) slices. Arrange the apple slices over the cake mixture in an overlapping pattern, starting from the edge of the tin.

Sprinkle the cinnamon and extra sugar over the top and bake for about 1 hour or until a skewer inserted into the middle comes out clean. Turn out onto a wire rack, turn the cake over and set aside to cool. Just before serving, brush the top of the cake with the warm apricot jam.

Orange and Passionfruit Cupcakes

MAKES 12

Kids love to help make, and eat, these little cakes. We usually top them with passionfruit icing (frosting) and a sprinkling of hundreds and thousands.

200 g (7 oz) unsalted butter, softened
1 tablespoon finely grated orange zest
1 teaspoon pure vanilla extract
200 g (7 oz) caster (superfine) sugar
pinch of salt
3 large eggs
pulp of 4 passionfruit
300 g (10½ oz/2 cups) self-raising flour, sifted
60 ml (2 fl oz/¼ cup) milk
185 g (6 oz/1½ cups) icing (confectioners') sugar
coloured sprinkles or glacé (candied) fruits, for decorating

Preheat the oven to 200°C (400°F). Line twelve 80 ml (3 fl oz/⅓ cup) muffin holes with cupcake cases.

Using electric beaters, beat the butter, orange zest, vanilla extract, caster sugar and salt until creamy. Beat in the eggs one at a time, mixing well. Add the pulp of one of the passionfruit. Gradually stir in the sifted flour, alternating with the milk.

Spoon or pipe the cake mixture into the prepared muffin holes, filling them a little over halfway.

Bake for 15–18 minutes or until firm to touch. Reduce the temperature if the cakes are browning too quickly. Set aside to cool.

Strain the pulp of the remaining passionfruit. Place the icing sugar in a bowl and gradually add the passionfruit pulp to give a thickish consistency. Using a small spatula, spread a little icing (frosting) over each cake and decorate with sprinkles or pieces of glacé fruit.

Poppyseed Cake

SERVES 8–10

We made this cake many times when our youngest son, Michael, was at school as it was one of his favourite lunchbox treats.

125 g (4 oz) unsalted butter, softened
finely grated zest of 1 lemon
1 tablespoon orange blossom honey or
    other honey
1 tablespoon lemon juice
285 g (10 oz/1¼ cups) caster (superfine)
    sugar
1 egg yolk
250 ml (8½ fl oz/1 cup) milk
250 g (9 oz/1⅔ cups) plain (all-purpose)
    flour, sifted
pinch of salt
2 teaspoons baking powder
60 g (2 oz) poppyseeds
4 egg whites

LEMON ICING
210 g (7 oz/1⅔ cups) icing (confectioners')
    sugar
juice of 1 lemon

Preheat the oven to 160°C (320°F). Butter a 20 cm (8 in) ring (bundt) tin.

Using electric beaters, beat the butter, lemon zest, honey, lemon juice and 225 g (8 oz/1 cup) of the sugar until creamy. Beat in the egg yolk and milk. Don't worry if the mixture looks a little curdled at this stage. Add the sifted flour, salt, baking powder and 4 tablespoons of the poppyseeds and mix well.

Beat the egg whites in a separate bowl until stiff peaks form. Add the remaining sugar and beat a little more. Gently fold the egg white mixture into the cake mixture, then pour into the prepared tin.

Bake for about 45 minutes or until a skewer inserted into the middle comes out clean. Set aside for 5 minutes before turning out onto a wire rack to cool completely.

To make the lemon icing (frosting), put the icing sugar in a bowl and gradually stir in enough lemon juice to give the icing a creamy consistency. You may not need all of the lemon juice.

Spread the icing over the cake and sprinkle with the remaining poppyseeds.

Poppyseed Cake

Chestnut and Chocolate Cake with Raspberries

SERVES 12

Chestnut cream is one of the most popular flavours for French people. I hope you will love it as much as we do.

250 g (9 oz) caster (superfine) sugar
8 large eggs
250 g (9 oz/1⅔ cups) plain (all-purpose) flour
2 tablespoons Dutch (unsweetened) cocoa powder
100 g (3½ oz) butter, just melted
100 g (3½ oz) raspberry jam
400 g (14 oz) can sweetened chestnut cream (crème de marrons)
250 ml (8½ fl oz/1 cup) cream, whipped until firm
½ quantity Chocolate Ganache (page 186)
300 g (10½ oz) raspberries

Preheat the oven to 180°C (350°F). Butter and flour a 25 cm (10 in) round cake tin.

Using electric beaters, beat the sugar and eggs in a large bowl until the mixture forms a thick ribbon.

Sift the flour with the cocoa, then add to the egg mixture all at once and, using a large metal spoon or rubber spatula, fold it into the mixture, gently but quickly. Stir in the melted butter.

Pour the mixture into the prepared tin and smooth the top. Bake for 30–40 minutes or until the cake springs back when lightly touched in the centre. Set aside for a few minutes before gently turning out onto a wire rack to cool.

Cut the sponge into three layers. Thinly spread the bottom two layers with raspberry jam.

Fold the chestnut cream into the whipped cream, then spread over the jam. Stack the sponge layers, placing the plain one on top. Ice the top with the chocolate ganache and decorate with the raspberries.

Soft-Centred Chocolate Cakes

SERVES 4

The secret to these little cakes is not to overcook them, so the centres remain soft.

150 g (5 oz/1 cup) dark chocolate, chopped
30 g (1 oz) butter, cut into cubes
2 egg yolks
20 g (¾ oz) plain (all-purpose) flour, sifted
3 egg whites
pinch of cream of tartar
55 g (2 oz/¼ cup) sugar
1 tablespoon dark chocolate bits
cream, ice cream or custard, to serve

Preheat the oven to 220°C (430°F). Butter four 185 ml (6 fl oz/³/₄ cup) soufflé dishes.

Place the chocolate in a microwave-safe bowl and microwave on high for 30 seconds. Stir the chocolate for a few seconds, then microwave for another 10 seconds. Stir again, then microwave for 10 seconds more. Stir again. Repeat until the chocolate is melted and smooth. Stir the butter into the melted chocolate until very smooth. Set aside to cool a little, then whisk in the egg yolks and sifted flour.

Using electric beaters, beat the egg whites and cream of tartar until stiff peaks form. Gradually beat in the sugar until well combined. Fold the egg whites into the chocolate mixture until combined.

Half fill the prepared dishes with the chocolate mixture. Place 1 teaspoon of chocolate bits in the centre of each, then top with the remaining mixture and smooth the top. Bake for about 10 minutes. The soufflés will rise and the centres will be soft.

Serve in the dishes or turn out onto plates. Serve warm with cream, ice cream or custard.

Rum Savarin with Tropical Fruits

SERVES 6–8

The *gâteau Savarin* — a yeast cake moistened with syrup — is a great French classic.

7–10 g (¼ oz) instant dry yeast

2 tablespoons warm milk

200 g (7 oz/1⅓ cups) plain (all-purpose)
  flour, sifted

3 large eggs

90 g (3 oz) unsalted butter, softened

330 g (12 oz/1½ cups) sugar

zest of 1 lemon

60 ml (2 fl oz/¼ cup) rum

2 mangoes

pulp of 2 passionfruit

lemon zest shavings, to decorate

Dissolve the yeast in the milk and set aside for 15 minutes.

Using electric beaters or a wooden spoon, beat the sifted flour, yeast mixture and eggs until the dough is elastic, about 2 minutes. Cover with a cloth and set aside to rise for about 1 hour.

Preheat the oven to 200°C (400°F). Butter a 20 cm (8 in) ring (bundt) tin.

Add the softened butter and 1 tablespoon of the sugar to the risen dough and beat thoroughly with a wooden spoon. Place the mixture in a piping bag and pipe into the prepared tin, tapping the tin lightly to eliminate any air bubbles. Set aside to rise in a warm place, uncovered, for 30 minutes. Bake for 25 minutes or until a bamboo skewer inserted into the middle comes out dry.

Meanwhile, bring 500 ml (17 fl oz/2 cups) water, the remaining sugar and lemon zest to the boil and cook for 5 minutes.

Remove the cake from the oven and set aside for about 3 minutes before turning it out onto a dish. Stir the rum into the sugar syrup and pour this over the cake. Allow the cake to absorb the syrup.

Peel and slice the mangoes and combine them with the passionfruit pulp. Spoon this mixture into the middle of the cake and decorate with shavings of lemon zest.

Hazelnut Meringue Cake with Chocolate Ganache

SERVES 8–10

The meringue and filling can be prepared a day or two in advance, then the cake can be assembled on the day you need it. The assembled cake keeps well for 36 hours.

80 g (3 oz/¾ cup) ground hazelnuts, toasted
1½ tablespoons cornflour (cornstarch)
240 g (9 oz) caster (superfine) sugar
6 large egg whites
pinch of cream of tartar
2 drops red wine vinegar
3 drops pure vanilla extract
40 roasted hazelnuts, chopped into small pieces
1 quantity Chocolate Ganache (page 186)
icing (confectioners') sugar, for dusting

Preheat the oven to 180°C (350°F). Draw a 20 cm (8 in) circle on three sheets of baking paper and use them to line three baking trays.

In a bowl combine the toasted ground hazelnuts, cornflour and one-quarter of the sugar.

Using electric beaters, beat the egg whites and cream of tartar on medium to high speed until almost stiff. Reduce speed to low, gradually add the remaining sugar, then the vinegar and vanilla extract, and beat until stiff peaks form.

Fold the hazelnut mixture into the beaten egg whites. Spoon into a piping bag fitted with a 1 cm (½ in) plain nozzle. Pipe three discs inside the circles on the baking paper, starting from the outside and moving inwards. Sprinkle half the roasted hazelnuts onto one of the discs. Bake the discs for 30 minutes or until the meringue is firm and dry. Set aside to cool.

Stir the remaining roasted hazelnuts into the chocolate ganache and spread one plain disc with almost half the ganache. Place the second plain disc on top and spread with ganache, reserving 2–3 tablespoons for the side of the cake. Top with the last disc, with the hazelnuts on top.

Briefly heat the remaining ganache until spreadable, then spread it over the side of the cake, using a spatula. Dust the cake with icing sugar to serve.

Carrot and Hazelnut Cake

MAKES ABOUT 12 SLICES

You will find that this cake is quick, easy to make and quite moist — a lovely cake for afternoon tea.

170 g (6 oz/¾ cup) caster (superfine) sugar

2 tablespoons maple syrup

3 eggs

185 ml (6 fl oz/¾ cup) lemon-flavoured olive oil

225 g (8 oz/1½ cups) wholemeal (whole-wheat) self-raising flour

1 teaspoon bicarbonate of soda (baking soda)

½ teaspoon ground cinnamon

pinch of salt

235 g (8½ oz/1½ cups) grated carrot

60 g (2 oz/½ cup) currants, sultanas (golden raisins) or raisins

70 g (2½ oz/½ cup) roasted hazelnuts, chopped

Preheat the oven to 180°C (350°F). Butter a 25 x 11 cm (10 x 4½ in) loaf (bar) tin and line with baking paper.

Put the sugar, maple syrup, eggs and olive oil in a large bowl and mix until thoroughly combined. Stir in the flour, bicarbonate of soda, cinnamon and salt until smooth, but don't overmix.

Stir in the carrot, currants and hazelnuts. Pour into the prepared tin and bake for about 1 hour or until a skewer inserted into the middle comes out clean. Set aside for 10 minutes before turning out onto a wire rack to cool.

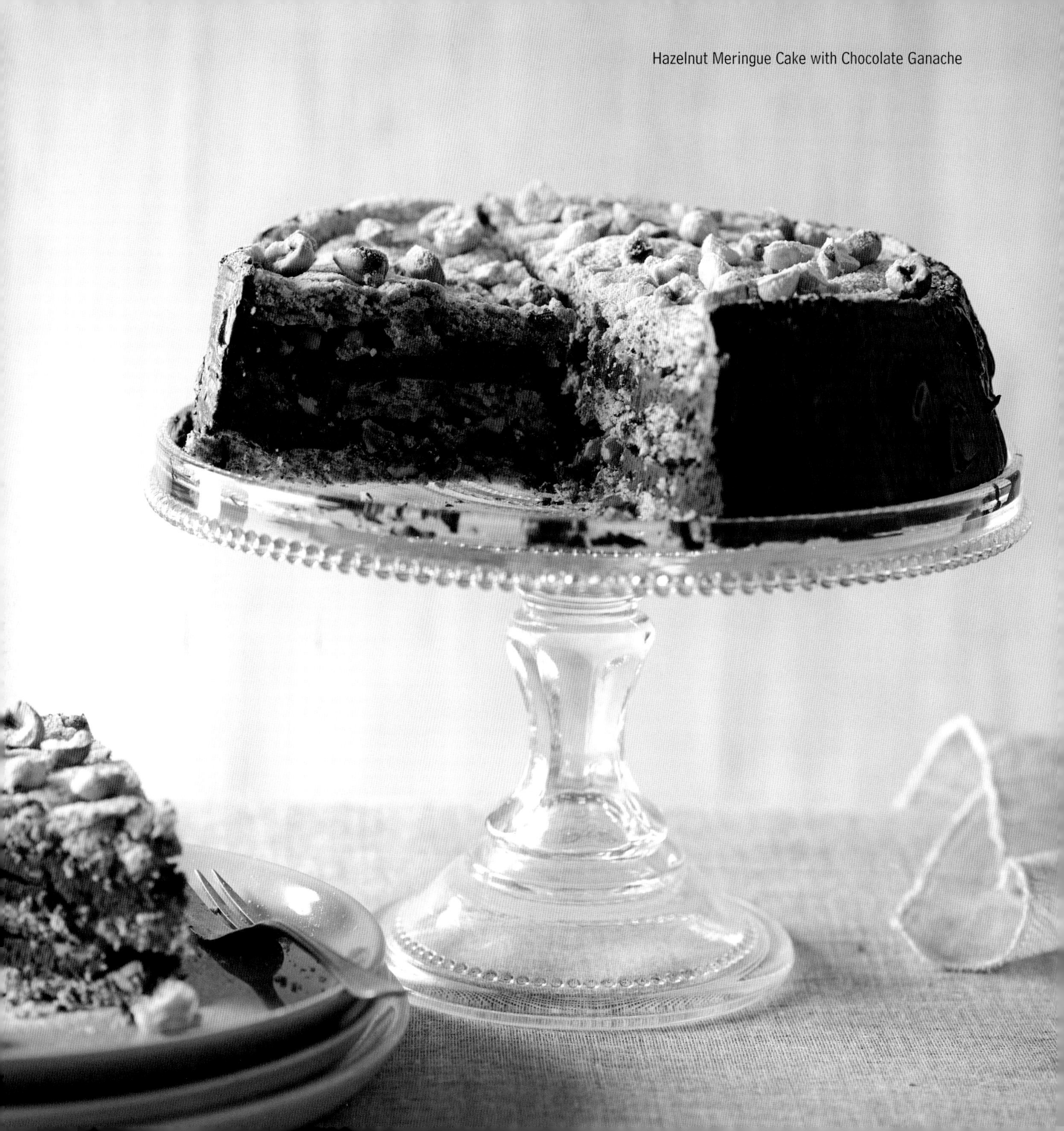
Hazelnut Meringue Cake with Chocolate Ganache

Apricot and Almond Cake

SERVES 6–8

I love making cakes and desserts using seasonal fruits. Apricots are one of my favourite fruits, and as the season is relatively short, I make sure I don't miss out when they are at the market.

10 ripe apricots
150 g (5 oz) butter, softened
145 g (5 oz/⅔ cup) caster (superfine) sugar
2 teaspoons finely grated lemon zest
3 eggs
120 g (4 oz) ground almonds
100 g (3½ oz/⅔ cup) self-raising flour, sifted
icing (confectioners') sugar, for dusting

Preheat the oven to 200°C (400°F). Butter and flour a 28 cm (11 in) flan tin.

Halve the apricots and remove the stones. Cut ten of the apricot halves in half again.

Using electric beaters, beat the butter, sugar and lemon zest for a few minutes or until creamy. Beat in the eggs, then stir in the ground almonds and sifted flour. Finally, stir in the apricot quarters.

Carefully pour the mixture into the prepared tin and tap the base to distribute the mixture evenly. Arrange the remaining apricot halves on top, then bake the cake for about 45 minutes or until a skewer inserted into the middle comes out clean. Set aside for 10 minutes before carefully turning out onto a wire rack to cool completely.

Dust the top with icing sugar just before serving.

Savoy Sponge

SERVES 10–12

The *gâteau de Savoie* is a classic French cake. It is usually served for afternoon tea with custard. Its beauty is in its simplicity.

90 g (3 oz/¾ cup) cornflour (cornstarch), sifted
90 g (3 oz) plain flour, sifted
6 eggs, separated
285 g (10 oz/1¼ cups) caster (superfine) sugar
grated zest of ½ lemon
pinch of cream of tartar
icing (confectioners') sugar for dusting
custard and seasonal fresh fruits, to serve

Preheat the oven to 180°C (350°F). Butter a 25 cm (10 in) round cake tin.

In a bowl, sift together the cornflour and plain flour.

Using electric beaters, beat the egg yolks with 145 g (5 oz/⅔ cup) of the sugar and the lemon zest until the mixture is light and creamy.

In a separate bowl, beat the egg whites and cream of tartar until stiff peaks form. Gradually beat in the remaining sugar. Gently fold the beaten whites into the egg-yolk mixture. Lastly, fold in the sifted flours, being careful not to overmix.

Pour the mixture into the prepared tin. Flatten the top and dust with a little icing sugar. Bake for about 35–40 minutes or until a skewer inserted into the middle comes out clean. Set aside for 10 minutes before carefully turning out onto a wire rack to cool completely.

Serve with custard and seasonal fresh fruits.

tarts and pies

Chocolate Tart

SERVES 8–10

A chocolate tart is always a superb treat and one I particularly enjoy in the afternoon.

1 quantity Sweet Pastry (page 176)
300 ml (10 fl oz) cream
180 g (6 oz) dark chocolate, chopped
1 large egg, lightly beaten
2 tablespoons Dutch (unsweetened) cocoa
     powder, for dusting

Preheat the oven to 200°C (400°F). Grease a 22 cm (8½ in) loose-based flan tin.

Briefly knead the pastry to soften it, then roll it out on a well-floured surface to a thickness of about 3 mm (⅛ in). Gently wrap the pastry around the rolling pin and lay it over the prepared tin. Line the tin with the pastry and trim the edges. Prick the base of the pastry with a fork.

Line the pastry with foil and fill with uncooked rice or dried beans. Bake the pastry for 10 minutes, then carefully remove the foil and its contents and cook for another 2–5 minutes or until the pastry is cooked and golden brown.

Meanwhile, bring the cream to the boil in a saucepan. Remove from the heat, add the chocolate and stir until melted. Whisk in the egg.

Pour the chocolate mixture into the pastry shell. Reduce the oven to 140°C (275°F) and bake the tart for about 15–20 minutes or until the chocolate has slightly set. Set aside until cold, then refrigerate until ready to serve. Dust the tart with cocoa powder just before serving.

Apple and Calvados Pie

SERVES 8

Calvados is an apple liqueur made in Normandy. It adds a special flavour to this great winter dessert.

4 apples, peeled, cored and halved
20 g (³⁄₄ oz) butter
55 g (2 oz/¹⁄₄ cup) caster (superfine) sugar
1¹⁄₂ tablespoons Calvados
1 tablespoon finely grated lemon zest
700 g (1¹⁄₂ lbs) Puff Pastry (page 180) or
    store-bought
1 egg yolk mixed with 1 teaspoon cold water
thick (double/heavy) cream, to serve

Preheat the oven to 180°C (350°F). Butter a 22 cm (8¹⁄₂ in) loose-based flan tin.

Cut the apple halves into 1 cm (³⁄₄ in) slices. Melt the butter in a large non-stick frying pan over medium heat. Add the sugar and stir until dissolved. Add the apple slices and cook, turning once, until caramelised on both sides.

Bring the Calvados to the boil in a small saucepan. Pour over the apple mixture and, using a match, very carefully light the Calvados. The flame will burn for a few seconds. Transfer the apples to a plate to cool. Stir in the lemon zest.

Cut the pastry in half and roll out both pieces on a floured surface to a thickness of 4 mm (¹⁄₄ in). Cut out two circles the size of the flan tin. Lay one pastry circle in the prepared tin. Brush around the pastry edges with the egg-yolk mixture and prick the base with a fork. Spoon the apple slices into the centre of the pastry, leaving a 2 cm (³⁄₄ in) border.

Place the remaining pastry on top of the apple slices and pinch the pastry edges together. Make a hole in the centre of the pastry using the tip of a knife and brush the top with the remaining egg yolk. Using a fork, make a crisscross pattern on top of the pastry. Refrigerate for 15 minutes.

Bake the pie for 30 minutes or until the pastry is golden brown. Set aside to cool before carefully removing from the tin. Cut the pie into wedges and serve with thick cream.

Mango and Passionfruit Tartlets

MAKES 12

Make the pastry shells and crème pâtissière ahead of time, if you wish. Avoid assembling the tartlets more than 2 hours before serving, otherwise the pastry will become soggy.

1 quantity Sweet Pastry or Sweet Pastry with Almonds (pages 176 to 177), chilled for at least 1 hour
2 mangoes
pulp of 6 passionfruit
60 ml (2 fl oz/$\frac{1}{4}$ cup) cream
1 quantity Crème Pâtissière (page 184)

Preheat the oven to 200°C (400°F). Place twelve 8 cm (3 in) tartlet tins on a baking tray.

Briefly knead the chilled pastry to soften it, then roll it out on a well-floured surface to a thickness of about 4 mm ($\frac{1}{4}$ in). Cut the pastry into squares to fit the tartlet tins. Line each tin with pastry, patting gently against the base and side, and trim the edge with your fingertips, taking care not to tear the pastry. Prick the base with a fork.

Bake the pastry shells for about 10 minutes or until the pastry is cooked and the edges are golden brown. Set aside to cool before removing from the tins.

Peel the mangoes and cut the flesh into small strips about 6 cm ($2\frac{1}{2}$ in) long and place in a bowl with the pulp of four of the passionfruit.

Stir the cream and remaining passionfruit pulp into the crème pâtissière. Place a spoonful in each pastry shell and spread it out a little. Arrange the mango mixture over the cream and refrigerate until ready to serve.

French Apple Tartlets

SERVES 6

This dessert brings back beautiful memories of my youth, cooking with my mum and grandmother at home. At its best, it's heaven.

6 Granny Smith apples
400 g (14 oz) Puff Pastry (page 180 or store-bought)
2 tablespoons thick (double/heavy) cream
1 tablespoon caster (superfine) sugar
70 g (2½ oz) smooth apricot jam, warmed

Preheat the oven to 230°C (450°F). Line a baking tray with baking paper.

Peel and core the apples and cut two of them into eight pieces each. Place the apple pieces in a saucepan with 2 tablespoons water, cover and cook for a few minutes or until tender. Mash the apple, then set aside to cool.

Roll out the pastry to a thickness of about 2 mm (⅛ in) and cut into six 8–10 cm (3–4 in) rounds. Place the rounds on the prepared tray and prick with a fork to prevent the pastry from shrinking. Refrigerate the pastry while you prepare the apples.

Halve the remaining apples and cut them into thin slices about 2 mm (⅛ in) thick.

Stir the cream into the mashed apple and spread it over the pastry, leaving a 1 cm (½ in) border. Overlap the apple slices on the pastry, working in a spiral pattern from the outside towards the centre, leaving no gaps.

Sprinkle the sugar over the tarts and bake for about 15 minutes or until the pastry is golden and crisp and the edges of the apple are lightly browned.

Lightly brush the tarts with the apricot jam and serve warm.

Raspberry and Passionfruit Tart

SERVES 8

This is one of my all-time favourite tarts. It's best made in spring and early summer when raspberries are sweet. This recipe will make two tarts.

400 g (14 oz) Puff Pastry (page 180 or
    store-bought)
1 egg yolk
2 teaspoons milk
2 tablespoons caster (superfine) sugar
90 g (3 oz) raspberry jam
200 ml (7 fl oz) thick (double/heavy) cream
pulp of 4 passionfruit
500 g (1 lb 2 oz) raspberries
icing (confectioners') sugar, for dusting

Preheat the oven to 220°C (430°F). Line a baking tray with baking paper.

Roll out the puff pastry to a 25 cm (10 in) square and place on the prepared tray. Prick the pastry with a fork to prevent it from shrinking. Whisk the egg yolk with the milk, then brush it over the pastry.

Cut the pastry in half. Cut two strips 5 mm ($\frac{1}{4}$ in) wide from each long side of the two pastry rectangles. Gently lay the strips along the edges of the rectangles. Sprinkle the pastry with caster sugar and bake for 15 minutes or until the pastry is cooked and dry. Reduce the oven temperature if the top is browning too much. Set aside to cool.

In a small saucepan briefly heat the raspberry jam to thin it, then brush the jam over the pastry. When cool, spread with the cream. Spoon the passionfruit pulp over the cream and top with the raspberries.

Dust with the icing sugar, cut each tart into four pieces and serve immediately.

Apricot Tart

SERVES 8–10

This is one of my absolute favourite desserts. My grandmother used to make it when I was a child. Prepare the pastry and crème pâtissière a day ahead, if you wish.

1 quantity Sweet Pastry with Almonds (page 177)
½ quantity Crème Pâtissière (page 184), chilled
2 tablespoons cream, whipped until firm
6–8 apricots, halved and stoned
2 tablespoons caster (superfine) sugar
60 g (2 oz) smooth apricot jam, warmed (optional)

Preheat the oven to 200°C (400°F). Grease a 35 cm (14 in) loose-based rectangular flan tin or 24 cm (9½ in) loose-based round flan tin.

Briefly knead the pastry to soften it, then roll it out on a well-floured surface to a thickness of about 4–5 mm (¼ in). Gently wrap the pastry around the rolling pin and lay it over the prepared tin. Line the tin with the pastry and trim the edges. Prick the base of the pastry with a fork.

Mix the cold crème pâtissière into the whipped cream and spread a thin layer over the pastry shell. Arrange the apricot halves, cut-side up, over the crème pâtissière, keeping them close together.

Dust the apricots with the sugar and bake the tart for about 35–40 minutes. If after 15–20 minutes the pastry or apricots look a little too brown, reduce the temperature to 150°C (300°F). The tart is cooked when the pastry is dry and golden brown.

Serve the tart warm or cold, glazed with a little warm apricot jam, if desired.

Apricot Tart

Pear and Almond Tart

SERVES 8–10

Make this sweet tart using just-ripe pears or, if you wish, use canned pears. You can use very finely chopped almonds instead of the ground almonds. The pastry base can be made in advance.

1 quantity Sweet Pastry (page 176)
4 pears
seeds of $\frac{1}{2}$ vanilla pod
115 g (4 oz/$\frac{1}{2}$ cup) caster (superfine) sugar
25 g (1 oz/$\frac{1}{4}$ cup) ground almonds
60 ml (2 fl oz/$\frac{1}{4}$ cup) cream
2 eggs
1 tablespoon brandy, Kirsch or Drambuie (optional)
70 g (2$\frac{1}{2}$ oz) smooth apricot jam, warmed

Preheat the oven to 220°C (430°F). Grease a 25 cm (10 in) loose-based flan tin.

Briefly knead the pastry to soften it, then roll it out on a floured surface to a thickness of 4 mm ($\frac{1}{4}$ in). Gently wrap the pastry around the rolling pin and lay it over the prepared tin. Line the tin with the pastry, and trim the edge. Prick the base of the pastry with a fork.

Line the pastry with foil and fill with uncooked rice or dried beans. Bake the pastry for 10 minutes, then carefully remove the foil and its contents and cook for another 2–5 minutes or until the pastry is dry and lightly browned. Remove from the oven and place the flan tin on a baking tray.

Peel, quarter and core the pears. Cut each quarter into slices about 1 cm ($\frac{1}{2}$ in) thick and arrange on top of the pastry.

Stir the vanilla seeds and sugar in a bowl. Add the ground almonds, cream, eggs and brandy, if using, and stir until well combined. Pour the mixture over the pear slices.

Place the tart in the oven, reduce the heat to 150°C (300°F) and bake for 25 minutes. Set aside to cool a little, then brush the top with the apricot jam. Remove from the tin and serve warm.

English-Style Apple Pie

SERVES 8

Everyone who enjoys cooking should learn to make an apple pie. It's so much fun and always popular.

4 Granny Smith apples, peeled and cored
seeds of ½ vanilla pod
1 tablespoon finely grated lemon zest
2 tablespoons brown sugar
¼ teaspoon ground cinnamon
3 teaspoons cornflour (cornstarch)
1 quantity Sweet Pastry (page 176)
1 egg yolk mixed with 1 teaspoon cold water
30 g (1 oz) butter, chopped

Preheat the oven to 220°C (430°F). Grease and line a 25 cm (10 in) flan tin.

Halve and thinly slice the apples. Place in a bowl with the vanilla seeds, lemon zest, brown sugar, cinnamon and cornflour. Toss to combine.

Cut the pastry into two pieces, making one piece twice as large as the other. Roll out the large piece on a floured surface to a thickness of 4 mm (¼ in). Gently wrap the pastry around the rolling pin and lay it over the prepared tin. Line the tin with the pastry, and trim the edge. Prick the base of the pastry with a fork. Brush the pastry with the egg-yolk mixture and top with the apple mixture. Dot the butter over the apple.

Roll out the remaining pastry on a floured surface until large enough to cover the top of the pie, then prick it a few times with a fork. Lay the pastry over the pie, trimming any excess dough. Pinch the top and sides together to seal the pie, then brush with the remaining egg yolk. You can use any leftover pastry to decorate the top of the pie.

Bake the pie for 10 minutes, then reduce the oven to 180°C (350°F) and bake for a further 30–35 minutes or until the pastry is dry and golden brown.

Cherry and Pistachio Tart

SERVES 8–10

You will need a cherry pitter for this special tart that I make in the early summer months. The pastry base can be made in advance. If you need to peel the pistachios, drop them in boiling water for 20 seconds, then drain and peel them.

1 quantity Sweet Pastry (page 176)
400 g (14 oz) cherries, pitted
60 g (2 oz) raw peeled pistachios
2 tablespoons walnut or olive oil
115 g (4 oz/½ cup) caster (superfine) sugar
½ vanilla pod, split lengthwise
125 ml (4 fl oz/½ cup) cream
2 eggs
1 tablespoon brandy, Kirsch or Drambuie
   (optional)
70 g (2½ oz) smooth apricot jam, warmed

Preheat the oven to 220°C (430°F). Grease a 25 cm (10 in) loose-based flan tin.

Briefly knead the pastry to soften it, then roll it out on a floured surface to a thickness of 3 mm (⅛ in). Gently wrap the pastry around the rolling pin and lay it over the prepared tin. Line the tin with the pastry and trim the edges. Prick the base of the pastry with a fork.

Line the pastry with foil and fill with uncooked rice or dried beans. Bake the pastry for 10 minutes, then carefully remove the foil and its contents and cook for another 2–5 minutes or until the pastry is lightly browned. Remove from the oven and place the flan tin on a baking tray.

Arrange the cherries on top of the pastry.

Using a food processor, blend the pistachios and oil into a rough paste.

Combine the sugar and vanilla pod in a bowl and mix for 1 minute. Stir in the pistachio paste, cream, eggs and brandy, if using, until well combined. Discard the vanilla pod, then pour the mixture over the cherries.

Place the tart in the oven, reduce the heat to 150°C (300°F) and bake for 25 minutes. Set aside to cool, then brush the top with apricot jam. Remove from the tin and serve warm.

Tarte Tatin

SERVES 6–8

The Tatin has to be one of the most well-loved French desserts. Take great care when you turn the tart out of the pan. I use a cast-iron skillet, but any heavy-based ovenproof frying pan will work well.

5–6 medium Golden Delicious apples
pinch of ground cinnamon
150 g (5 oz) sugar
50 g (2 oz) butter
350 g (12 oz) Puff Pastry (page 180 or
    store-bought)

Preheat the oven to 220°C (430°F).

Peel, core and quarter the apples, then sprinkle with the cinnamon.

Put the sugar and butter in a 20 cm (8 in) heavy-based ovenproof frying pan. Add the apple quarters, tightly packing them in a single layer.

Place the frying pan over medium heat and cook the apples for 10 minutes or until the caramel in the bottom of the pan is just beginning to turn golden brown and the apples are soft. If the apples are still firm, place the pan in the oven for about 2 minutes. Don't worry if there seems to be a lot of juice in the pan — it will be absorbed by the apples during baking.

Roll out the pastry to a circle a little larger than the pan, about 5 mm (¼ in) thick. Prick the pastry with a fork. Place the pastry on top of the apples and ease it down between the apples and the side of the pan.

Bake the tart for 15–20 minutes or until the pastry is dry and golden brown. Set aside for 10 minutes. Place an upside-down serving plate on top of the pan and hold it against the pan as you carefully invert the pan and unmould the tart. Serve warm or cold.

crèmes and mousses

Chocolate Mousse

SERVES 6

As a boy this was one of my five favourite desserts — along with crème caramel, fruit tarts, floating islands and ice cream. I still love it.

150 g (5 oz/1 cup) dark chocolate, chopped
80 g (3 oz) unsalted butter, chopped
2 egg yolks
1 teaspoon instant coffee (optional)
3 egg whites
pinch of cream of tartar
2 tablespoons icing (confectioners') sugar
6 strawberries, to serve
grated dark chocolate, to serve

Place the chocolate in a heatproof bowl over a saucepan of simmering water. Whisk slowly until smooth, then remove from the heat. Whisk the butter into the melted chocolate, then add the egg yolks and coffee, if using, and whisk until smooth.

Using electric beaters, beat the egg whites and cream of tartar until fairly firm. Add the icing sugar and continue beating until stiff peaks form.

Using a large metal spoon, gently incorporate a quarter of the egg whites into the chocolate mixture, then carefully fold in the remaining egg whites. Gently spoon the mixture into a bowl and refrigerate for several hours or until set.

Serve the mousse with the strawberries, sprinkled with grated chocolate.

Persimmon and Raspberry Mousse

SERVES 4

Each year I can't wait for the persimmon season. This delicate dinner-party dessert is sure to impress your guests. You will need four 10 cm (4 in) PVC rings that are about 4 cm (1½ in) high, available from plumbing-supply stores.

2 gelatine leaves
juice of 1 lemon
juice of ½ orange
350 g (12 oz) raspberries
½ vanilla pod, split lengthwise
100 g (3½ oz) caster (superfine) sugar
2 egg whites
pinch of cream of tartar
120 ml (4 fl oz) cream, whipped until firm
4 persimmons, peeled and cut into 1 cm
   (½ in) cubes
icing (confectioners') sugar, for dusting

Place the gelatine leaves in a large bowl, cover with cold water and set aside for about 15 minutes.

Place the lemon juice, orange juice, 150 g (5 oz) of the raspberries and the vanilla pod in a small saucepan. Bring to the boil and cook for 5 minutes, then strain into a bowl.

Squeeze out any water from the gelatine leaves. Mix the gelatine into the raspberry mixture, then set aside to cool.

Combine the sugar and 1½ tablespoons water in a saucepan and bring to a simmer. When the syrup reaches almost 120°C (250°F) on a sugar thermometer, use electric beaters to beat the egg whites and cream of tartar until stiff peaks form. Slowly pour the hot syrup onto the beaten egg whites and continue beating for about 8 minutes or until the mixture is almost cold. Using a large spoon, carefully fold in the cold raspberry mixture, then the whipped cream.

Place four 10 cm (4 in) PVC rings that are about 4 cm (1½ in) high on four serving plates. Spoon the cubed persimmons into the rings and top with the raspberry mousse. Gently smooth the top, then refrigerate for at least 2 hours to set.

Carefully run a blade around the inside of each ring. Top the mousse with the remaining raspberries and dust with icing sugar. Carefully lift off the rings and serve immediately.

Rice Pudding with Glacé Fruits and Chocolate Cream

SERVES 8

This is a satisfying family dessert. If you wish, replace the pineapple and apricot with other glacé (candied) fruits. You can make the dessert ahead of time.

140 g (4½ oz/⅔ cup) short-grain rice
875 ml (30 fl oz/3½ cups) milk
55 g (2 oz/¼ cup) caster (superfine) sugar
1 tablespoon grated orange zest
2 glacé (candied) pineapple rings, diced
4 glacé (candied) apricot pieces, diced
35 g (1½ oz/¼ cup) pistachios, finely chopped
250 ml (8½ fl oz/1 cup) cream, whipped
   until firm

CHOCOLATE CREAM
100 ml (3½ fl oz) milk
150 ml (5 fl oz) cream
180 g (6 oz) dark chocolate, grated

Place the rice in a saucepan and cover with plenty of cold water. Bring to the boil and cook for 4 minutes, then drain.

Bring the milk to the boil in a large saucepan. Stir in the rice, cover and simmer very gently, stirring once or twice, for about 30 minutes, after which time the mixture should be creamy. Pay attention during the last few minutes of cooking to ensure that the rice does not stick or burn.

Stir the sugar, orange zest and glacé fruits into the rice until well combined. Pour into a large bowl and set aside to cool. Fold the pistachios and whipped cream into the cold rice. Carefully spoon into eight glasses and refrigerate.

To make the chocolate cream, combine the milk and cream in a saucepan. Bring to the boil, then turn off the heat. Place all but 2 tablespoons of the grated chocolate in a heatproof bowl. Pour the hot milk mixture onto the grated chocolate and whisk until creamy. Set aside to cool a little.

Spoon the chocolate cream onto the rice pudding, cover with plastic wrap and refrigerate for at least 3 hours.

Just before serving, sprinkle the puddings with the remaining grated chocolate.

Floating Islands

SERVES 6

Floating Islands, *Oeufs à la Neige* or *Ile Flottante*, was one of my grandmother's favourite desserts. It's important to use very fresh eggs to make the poached meringue.

500 ml (17 fl oz/2 cups) milk
½ vanilla pod, split lengthwise
5 large eggs, separated
170 g (6 oz/¾ cup) caster (superfine) sugar
pinch of cream of tartar
100 g (3½ oz) flaked almonds, toasted
icing (confectioners') sugar, for dusting

CARAMEL
200 g (7 oz) sugar
1 teaspoon red wine vinegar

In a saucepan, bring the milk and vanilla pod to the boil.

Whisk the egg yolks with 125 g (4 oz) of the caster sugar until the mixture turns pale and forms a ribbon.

Pour the hot milk onto the egg-yolk mixture and whisk well. Pour into the saucepan and, using a wooden spatula, stir over medium heat until the custard thickens slightly and coats the back of the spatula. Do not allow the custard to boil. Strain into a heatproof bowl, then set aside to cool.

Beat the egg whites and cream of tartar until fairly firm. Beat in the remaining caster sugar until stiff peaks form.

Three-quarters fill a wide saucepan with water and bring to a simmer. Using a large metal spoon, scoop out six balls of the egg-white mixture and gently place them on top of the simmering water. Cook for 1 minute, then carefully turn them over and cook for a further 2–3 minutes. Lift the egg-white balls out of the water, and drain on a clean cloth.

Pour the cooled custard into a wide bowl. Gently place the egg-white balls on top of the custard and sprinkle with the flaked almonds.

Cook the sugar, vinegar and 2 tablespoons water in a small saucepan over medium heat for 5 minutes or until the mixture is light brown. Spoon the caramel over the top of the egg-white balls and dust with icing sugar. Serve immediately.

Chocolate Charlotte with Raspberries

SERVES 8–10

A charlotte is popular at the end of a dinner party. It looks fantastic presented at the table and your guests can choose exactly how much they would like.

500 ml (17 fl oz/2 cups) milk
½ vanilla pod, split lengthwise
20 g (¾ oz) powdered gelatine
6 egg yolks
150 g (5 oz) sugar
200 g (7 oz/1⅓) dark chocolate, chopped
20 Sponge Finger Biscuits (page 181) or
    store-bought
500 ml (17 fl oz/2 cups) cream, whipped
    until firm
100 g (3½ oz) dark chocolate, grated
500 g (1 lb 2 oz) raspberries
icing (confectioners') sugar, for dusting

Warm the milk and vanilla in a 3 litre (101 fl oz) saucepan.

Meanwhile, stir the gelatine into 60 ml (2 fl oz/¼ cup) cold water.

Using electric beaters, beat the egg yolks and sugar until light and fluffy. Pour the warm milk onto the egg mixture, whisking to combine quickly. Return the custard to the pan and stir continuously over medium heat, tracing a figure eight with a wooden spatula until the mixture coats the back of the spatula. This will take a few minutes. Strain the custard into a heatproof bowl. Whisk in the chopped chocolate until melted. Add the gelatine mixture and mix well, then set the custard aside to cool.

Meanwhile, line the base and side of a 2 litre (68 fl oz) charlotte mould with the sponge finger biscuits, cutting them to fit.

Fold the whipped cream into the cold chocolate custard. Spoon into the mould (there may be some custard left over) and refrigerate for about 4 hours or until set.

Carefully unmould the chilled charlotte out onto a serving plate, sprinkle with the grated chocolate. Dust with icing sugar and serve with the raspberries.

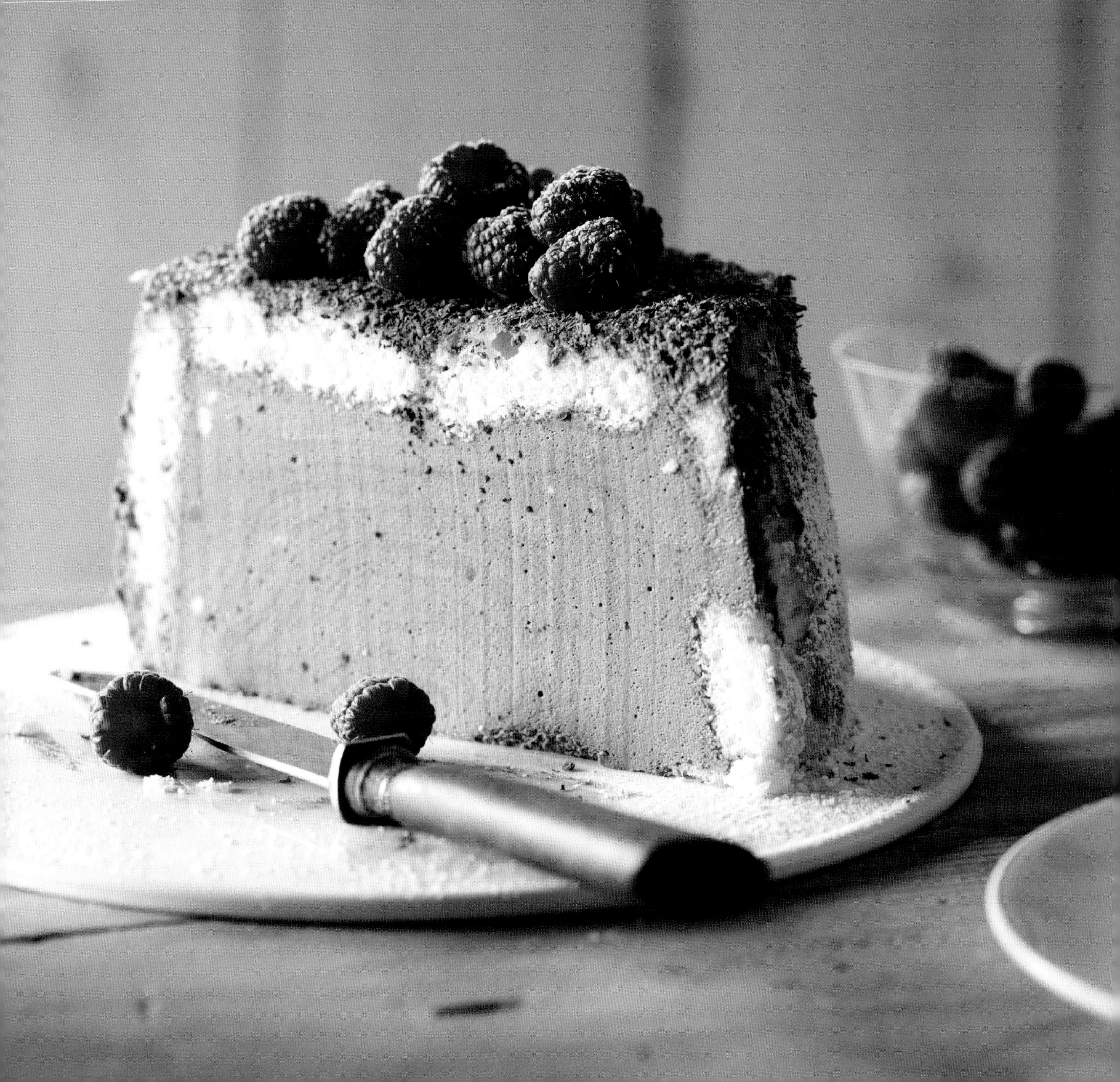

Crème Caramel

SERVES 8

This classic French dessert is popular with everybody and costs little to prepare. Concentrate well on cooking the caramel, which must turn a rich golden colour but not burn. They are usually best served the following day.

CARAMEL
200 g (7 oz) sugar
1 teaspoon red wine vinegar

1 litre (34 fl oz/4 cups) milk
½ vanilla pod or 2 drops pure vanilla extract
200 g (7 oz) caster (superfine) sugar
6 large eggs

Preheat the oven to 180°C (350°F).

To make the caramel, place the sugar, 2 tablespoons water and the vinegar in a small saucepan. Bring to the boil and cook until the caramel is a rich golden brown, taking care not to burn it. Immediately pour a little caramel into eight 185 ml (6 fl oz/¾ cup) ramekins, tilting to coat the base and a little way up the side.

Combine the milk and vanilla pod or extract in a saucepan and bring to the boil.

Meanwhile, place the sugar and eggs in a bowl and use a whisk to combine well. Pour the boiling milk onto the egg mixture and whisk well, then pass through a fine strainer into a jug.

Pour the egg mixture into the caramel-coated ramekins. Place the ramekins in a roasting tin and pour in enough warm water to come one-third of the way up the side of the tin. Carefully place the tin in the top part of the oven and cook for 30–40 minutes or until the crème is set but wobbles when lightly shaken. Set aside to cool before placing in the fridge to chill.

To serve, pass a blade around the sides of the ramekins and turn out each crème and its caramel onto a plate.

Mandarin Panna Cotta

SERVES 12

I love the aroma and taste of mandarin and in a panna cotta it's superb. Finely grate the mandarin rind, avoiding the white pith. I've suggested serving the panna cotta with a raspberry coulis, but you could use any of the fruit sauces on pages 187 to 189.

3 gelatine leaves
625 ml (21 fl oz/2$\frac{1}{2}$ cups) cream
375 ml (13 fl oz/1$\frac{1}{2}$ cups) milk
3 tablespoons very finely grated mandarin zest
145 g (5 oz/$\frac{2}{3}$ cup) caster (superfine) sugar
seeds of $\frac{1}{2}$ vanilla pod
1 quantity Raspberry Coulis (page 189)

Soak the gelatine leaves in a bowl of very cold water for a few minutes.

Place half the cream, all of the milk, grated mandarin zest, sugar and vanilla seeds in a saucepan and heat until almost boiling. Transfer the mixture to a heatproof bowl.

Squeeze out any water from the gelatine leaves. Whisk the gelatine into the mandarin cream, then set aside to cool.

Whip the remaining cream into soft peaks, then fold it into the mandarin mixture.

Pour the mixture into twelve 125 ml (4 fl oz/$\frac{1}{2}$ cup) dariole moulds and refrigerate for 4–5 hours or until set.

Spoon a little raspberry coulis onto twelve plates. Carefully turn out the panna cotta into the centre of the plates and serve with the remaining raspberry coulis.

Crémets d'Anjou with Raspberry Coulis

SERVES 6

This delicate dessert made with cream and a fresh soft cheese called fromage blanc is a speciality of my native region of Anjou in France.

200 ml (7 fl oz) cream
2 egg whites
pinch of cream of tartar
75 g (2½ oz) caster (superfine) sugar
250 g (9 oz) fromage blanc (smooth quark)
juice of ½ lemon
1 quantity Raspberry Coulis (page 189)
300 g (10½ oz) raspberries
icing (confectioners' sugar), for dusting

Place six 25 cm (10 in) square pieces of muslin into boiling water for 1 minute, then drain. This will rid the muslin of any impurities.

Beat the cream until it just starts to stiffen.

Using electric beaters, beat the egg whites and cream of tartar until stiff peaks form. Add 2 tablespoons of the sugar and continue beating until the egg whites are smooth and well combined.

Beat the fromage blanc with the remaining sugar and the lemon juice. Fold in the whipped cream, then gently fold in the beaten egg whites.

Place a square of muslin on a plate. Spoon one-sixth of the mixture into the centre, then lift the edges of the muslin to firmly wrap the contents. Tie the parcel with kitchen string and place on a wire rack over a tray to drain. Make the remaining five parcels, then refrigerate the parcels on the rack for at least 2–3 hours or overnight.

Carefully unmould the crémets onto dessert plates. Spoon a little of the raspberry coulis around each and top with the raspberries. Dust with icing sugar just before serving.

Mandarin Mousse with Blackcurrant Coulis

SERVES 6–8

A lovely way to finish a fine dinner, this mousse is out of this world.

100 g (3½ oz) caster (superfine) sugar
juice of 6 mandarins
juice of 1 lemon
finely grated zest of ½ lemon
10 g (½ oz) powdered gelatine
3 egg whites
pinch of cream of tartar
100 ml (3½ fl oz) cream, whipped until firm
1 quantity Blackcurrant Coulis (page 188) or
    Raspberry Coulis (page 189)
icing (confectioners') sugar, for dusting
mint leaves, to serve (optional)

Place two-thirds of the sugar, the mandarin juice, lemon juice and lemon zest in a saucepan. Bring to a simmer and cook for about 5 minutes or until reduced by more than half.

Transfer the mandarin mixture to a heatproof bowl. Whisk in the gelatine until dissolved, then set aside to cool.

Using electric beaters, beat the egg whites and cream of tartar until stiff peaks form. Beat in the remaining sugar until combined.

Whisk the whipped cream into the mandarin mixture. Gently fold in the beaten egg whites until just combined.

Transfer the mousse to a large serving bowl or individual moulds or glasses. Refrigerate for at least 2–3 hours to set.

Serve the mousse with the coulis, dusted with icing sugar and garnished with mint leaves, if using. It is also lovely with fresh fruits.

Creamy Coffee Custards

SERVES 8

I learned to make these delicious pots of flavoured custard as a young chef in Paris. In France they're called *petits pots de crème au café*.

2 tablespoons cream
800 ml (27 fl oz) milk
2 teaspoons coffee extract or 3 teaspoons instant coffee dissolved in 1 tablespoon hot water
2 large eggs plus 6 large egg yolks
145 g (5 oz/⅔ cup) caster (superfine) sugar
Dutch (unsweetened) cocoa powder, for dusting (optional)

Preheat the oven to 180°C (350°F).

Bring the cream and milk to the boil in a heavy-based saucepan. Stir in the coffee extract.

Using a whisk, beat the eggs, egg yolks and sugar in a mixing bowl until well combined. Stir in the hot milk mixture. Strain into a jug, then pour the mixture into eight 150 ml (5 fl oz) ramekins.

Place the ramekins in a roasting tin and three-quarters fill the tin with boiling water. Cover the top of the ramekins with greaseproof paper or baking paper.

Carefully place the tin in the oven and cook the custards for about 25 minutes or until just set. Set aside to cool, then refrigerate for at least 4 hours. Serve dusted with a little cocoa powder, if you wish.

Crème Brûlée

SERVES 6

This has become perhaps the most popular French dessert in the world.

250 ml (8½ fl oz/1 cup) cream (40% fat)
200 ml (7 fl oz) milk
1 vanilla pod, split lengthwise
4 egg yolks
120 g (4 oz/½ cup) caster (superfine) sugar
30 g (1 oz) brown sugar

Preheat the oven to 140°C (275°F).

Combine the cream, milk and vanilla pod in a saucepan. Bring to a simmer, then turn off the heat and set aside for 30 minutes.

Combine the egg yolks with 80 g (3 oz) of the caster sugar in a bowl. Stir in the milk mixture. Strain into a jug, then pour the mixture into six 185 ml (6 fl oz/¾ cup) ramekins.

Place the ramekins in a roasting tin and two-thirds fill the tin with hot water. Carefully place the tin in the oven and cook for 40 minutes. Remove from the oven and set aside to cool in the liquid. Refrigerate when cold.

Mix the remaining caster sugar with the brown sugar, then sprinkle evenly over the crèmes. Place the crèmes under a hot grill (broiler) until the sugar has caramelised, then serve immediately.

Tiramisu

SERVES 8–10

This is one of my favourite desserts ever — *grazie* to the Italians! In this variation of the classic recipe I use liqueur muscat instead of Marsala. Make your coffee from freshly ground coffee beans for the best result.

180 ml (6 fl oz/¾ cup) cold strong coffee

80 ml (3 fl oz/⅓ cup) liqueur muscat or Marsala

3 large eggs, separated

small pinch of cream of tartar

80 g (3 oz/⅓ cup) caster (superfine) sugar

seeds from ½ vanilla pod

300 g (10½ oz) fresh mascarpone cheese

18 Sponge Finger Biscuits (page 181 or store-bought)

2 tablespoons Dutch (unsweetened) cocoa powder, for dusting

Mix the coffee with half the muscat in a shallow bowl.

Using electric beaters, beat the egg whites and cream of tartar until stiff peaks form.

Using a whisk, beat the egg yolks, sugar and vanilla seeds until creamy.

Mix the remaining muscat with the mascarpone cheese, then gently stir into the egg-yolk mixture. Fold in the beaten egg whites.

Spoon about one-third of the mascarpone mixture into a wide serving bowl or individual serving glasses. Briefly dip the biscuits, one at a time, into the coffee and muscat and place a layer of biscuits on top of the mascarpone mixture. Repeat the layers, finishing with a layer of the mascarpone mixture. Cover with plastic wrap and refrigerate for at least 3 hours.

Dust the top of the tiramisu with cocoa powder just before serving.

Passionfruit Mousse and Mango Verrine

SERVES 8

This exotic dessert is served in a glass, *verre* in French. I think this is a perfect Christmas dessert.

pulp of 12 passionfruit
10 g (½ oz) powdered gelatine
150 g (5 oz) sugar
3 egg whites
pinch of cream of tartar
2 mangoes, peeled and cut into 1 cm (½ in) cubes
200 ml (7 fl oz) cream, whipped until firm

Heat 200 ml (7 fl oz) of the passionfruit pulp in a small saucepan, without boiling. Remove the pan from the heat and whisk in the gelatine until dissolved.

Place the sugar and 50 ml (2 fl oz) water in a small saucepan and bring to the boil. Place a sugar thermometer in the pan and cook over medium heat for 7–10 minutes or until the temperature reaches 121°C (250°F). Remove from the heat immediately. If you don't have a sugar thermometer, cook the sugar and water over medium heat for about 8 minutes or until the colour is slightly yellow. When you dip a teaspoon of the syrup into cold water, it should harden a little.

Using electric beaters, beat the egg whites and cream of tartar until stiff peaks form. Continue beating at low speed while you very slowly pour the syrup in a thin stream over the whites, taking care not to let it run into the beater whisk. Beat for about 8 minutes or until the mixture is almost completely cold. Fold in the passionfruit mixture and half of the diced mango.

Fold the whipped cream into the passionfruit mixture, then spoon into eight glasses, leaving at least 1 cm (½ in) at the top for the garnish. Cover with plastic wrap and refrigerate for at least 4 hours.

Toss together the remaining diced mango and passionfruit pulp. Spoon on top of the mousse and serve immediately.

Orange and Chocolate Crèmes

SERVES 10

When I was a boy, this classic French dessert was popular with children in restaurants.

60 g (2 oz/⅓ cup) dark chocolate chips
750 ml (25 fl oz/3 cups) milk
250 ml (8½ fl oz/1 cup) cream
4 tablespoons very finely grated orange zest
½ vanilla pod, split lengthwise
10 egg yolks
200 g (7 oz) caster (superfine) sugar

Preheat the oven to 180°C (350°F).

Sprinkle the chocolate chips into ten 185 ml (6 fl oz/¾ cup) ramekins.

Combine the milk, cream, orange zest and vanilla pod in a heavy-based saucepan and bring to the boil.

Using a whisk, beat the egg yolks and sugar in a mixing bowl until just combined.

Discard the vanilla pod and stir the hot milk into the egg-yolk mixture. Strain the mixture into a jug and pour into the ramekins.

Place the ramekins in a roasting tin and three-quarters fill the tin with boiling water. Cover the top of the ramekins with greaseproof paper or baking paper.

Place the tin in the oven and cook for 25 minutes or until the crèmes are just set. Set aside to cool, then refrigerate.

Serve the crèmes in the ramekins. They are lovely just on their own.

Chocolate Pearl Couscous Pudding with Coffee Cream

SERVES 6

This is a great dessert for chocolate lovers. The contrast between the coffee cream, the crunchy hazelnuts and the chocolate couscous is lovely. It looks great in whisky glasses.

250 ml (8½ fl oz/1 cup) milk
95 g (3½ oz) pearl (Israeli) couscous
2 tablespoons sugar
200 ml (7 fl oz) cream
80 g (3 oz) dark chocolate, chopped
2 teaspoons brandy or rum
½ teaspoon coffee extract or 1 teaspoon instant coffee
20 roasted hazelnuts, each chopped into 2 or 3 pieces
icing (confectioners') sugar, for dusting

Place the milk, pearl couscous and half the sugar in a saucepan. Bring to a simmer and cook for 11 minutes or until the couscous is cooked.

Stir in 80 ml (3 fl oz/⅓ cup) of the cream and return to a simmer, then remove from the heat. Transfer the mixture to a large bowl and gently stir in the chocolate until melted and well combined. Set aside to cool.

Whip the remaining cream and remaining sugar together until firm. Fold half of the whipped cream into the cold couscous mixture. Spoon into a piping bag without a nozzle and pipe into six serving glasses.

Mix the brandy with the coffee and whisk into the remaining whipped cream. Transfer to a piping bag fitted with a 1 cm (½ in) serrated nozzle. Pipe the coffee cream on top of the puddings, sprinkle with the chopped hazelnuts and dust with icing sugar. Serve immediately.

Blood Orange Mousse

SERVES 6

This delicate mousse contains an Italian meringue made from beaten egg whites and a sugar syrup. You can serve it with fresh fruits, such as strawberries, raspberries and blueberries.

200 ml (7 fl oz) blood orange juice
10 g (½ oz) powdered gelatine
juice of 1 lemon
150 g (5 oz) sugar
3 egg whites
pinch of cream of tartar
200 ml (7 fl oz) cream, whipped until firm
seasonal fresh fruits, such as strawberries,
    raspberries and blueberries, to serve

Heat the blood orange juice in a saucepan until hot but not boiling. Remove from the heat and whisk in the gelatine until it has dissolved. Stir in the lemon juice.

Place the sugar and 50 ml (2 fl oz) water in a small saucepan and bring to the boil over medium heat. Cook for 7–10 minutes or until the temperature reaches 121°C (250°F) on a sugar thermometer. Remove from the heat immediately. If you don't have a sugar thermometer, cook the sugar and water over medium heat for about 8 minutes or until the colour is slightly yellow. When you dip a teaspoon of the syrup into cold water, it should harden a little.

Using electric beaters, beat the egg whites and cream of tartar until stiff peaks form. Continue beating at low speed while you very slowly pour the syrup in a thin stream over the egg whites, taking care not to let it run into the beater whisk. Beat for about 8 minutes or until the mixture is almost completely cold. Fold in the blood-orange mixture.

Fold the whipped cream into the blood-orange mixture, then spoon into six moulds or glasses. Refrigerate for at least 3 hours before serving with your choice of seasonal fresh fruits.

fruits

Cherry and Mango Fruit Salad

SERVES 6

I often serve this noble fruit salad in early summer. You can serve it in individual glasses or from the centre of the table.

250 g (9 oz) raspberries or strawberries
juice of 1 orange
juice of ½ lemon
2 tablespoons caster (superfine) sugar
2 tablespoons Kirsch
350 g (12 oz) cherries, pitted
2 large mangoes, peeled and sliced
65 g (2½ oz) chopped almonds
6 scoops Vanilla Ice Cream (page 128 or
    store-bought)

In a food processor, blend the raspberries or strawberries to a purée with the orange juice, lemon juice and sugar. Strain into a bowl and stir in the Kirsch.

Add the cherries to the fruit purée and stir well.

Gently stir the mango slices and chopped almonds into the fruit purée. Serve with a scoop of ice cream.

Summer Pudding

SERVES 6–8

Summer pudding is a magnificent classic and it's always nice if you can include some raspberries and blackberries or blueberries. Strawberries don't work very well.

2 tablespoons caster (superfine) sugar
seeds of ½ vanilla pod
300 g (10½ oz) blackberries
300 g (10½ oz) blueberries
500 g (1 lb 2 oz) raspberries
1 sliced loaf raisin bread, brioche or panettone
extra berries, to serve
cream, to serve

Combine the sugar, vanilla seeds and 60 ml (2 fl oz/¼ cup) water in a large saucepan and heat until the sugar has dissolved. Add the berries and bring just to the boil, then remove from the heat.

Line the side of a 2 litre (68 fl oz) pudding basin with the slices of raisin bread, trimming any slices that are too large. Trim a slice to fit the base.

Pour the berries and juice into the lined pudding basin. Neatly arrange the remaining slices of trimmed raisin bread over the berries to form a lid. Cover the basin with plastic wrap. Place a plate that is slightly smaller than the basin on top to weigh it down. Refrigerate overnight.

To serve, invert the pudding onto a large serving plate and lift off the basin. Serve with extra berries and cream.

Poached Rhubarb and Quince on a Bed of Creamy Quark

SERVES 8

This delicious autumn dessert is lovely at the end of a dinner party. Most of the preparation can be done ahead.

515 g (1 lb 2 oz/2¼ cups) caster (superfine) sugar
finely grated zest of 1 lemon
1 vanilla pod, halved and split lengthwise
juice of 1 lemon
4 quinces, peeled, quartered and cored
8 rhubarb stalks
400 g (14 oz) quark cheese
150 ml (5 fl oz) cream
80 ml (3 fl oz/⅓ cup) milk
1 quantity Raspberry Coulis (page 189)
4 Meringues (page 182), each broken into 6–8 pieces

In a saucepan, combine 500 ml (17 fl oz/2 cups) water, 335 g (12 oz/1½ cups) of the sugar, half the lemon zest, half the vanilla pod and the lemon juice. Bring to a simmer, then cook for 5 minutes.

Cut each quince quarter into five thin wedges and add them to the syrup. Simmer for 10–15 minutes or until the quince wedges are tender. Set the quinces and syrup aside to cool, then refrigerate.

In a wide saucepan, combine 125 ml (4 fl oz/½ cup) water with 110 g (4 oz/½ cup) of the sugar, the remaining lemon zest and vanilla pod and bring to the boil.

Peel the hard part of the rhubarb stalks. Cut the rhubarb into 5 cm (2 in) pieces and add to the pan. Cover and cook until the rhubarb is just soft. Set aside to cool, then refrigerate.

Just before serving, beat the quark cheese with the remaining sugar, cream and milk until smooth and combined.

Spread 2–3 tablespoons of the quark mixture on eight plates. Drain the quince segments and place on top of the quark mixture with the rhubarb. Drizzle the raspberry coulis over the fruit, sprinkle with pieces of meringue and serve.

Pears Belle Hélène

SERVES 6

This is one of the first classic French desserts I learned to make during my chef's apprenticeship in the Anjou region of France. The region is famous for its pears, and our back garden was ringed with at least ten pear trees. You can use canned pear halves as a short-cut.

200 g (7 oz) sugar
½ vanilla pod, split lengthwise
6 pears
½ lemon (optional)
150 ml (5 fl oz) cream
200 g (7 oz/1⅓ cups) dark chocolate, chopped
1 litre (34 fl oz/4 cups) Vanilla Ice Cream
    (page 128 or store-bought)
100 g (3½ oz) flaked almonds, toasted,
    to serve
icing (confectioners') sugar, for dusting

Combine 1.5 litres (51 fl oz) water, the sugar and vanilla pod in a saucepan. Bring to the boil, then reduce the heat and simmer for 5 minutes.

Peel the pears. If they begin to discolour, rub them with the lemon half and place them in a bowl of cold water. Add the peeled pears to the simmering syrup and simmer for 15 minutes. Remove the pan from the heat and set aside for the pears to cool in the liquid.

Bring the cream to the boil in a small saucepan. Remove from the heat and stir in the chocolate until smooth. Set aside to cool a little.

Drain the pears and place in a bowl with one or two scoops of ice cream. Spoon a little chocolate sauce over the top, sprinkle with the toasted almonds and dust with icing sugar. Serve immediately.

Stewed Cherries with Strawberries and Apricots

SERVES 6

You can serve this yummy fruit concoction either on its own or with a selection of desserts at Christmas and festive occasions. It is also good with cream or ice cream.

250 ml (8½ fl oz/1 cup) fresh orange juice
juice of 1 lemon
100 g (3½ oz) sugar
1 vanilla pod, split lengthwise
6 ripe apricots, halved and stoned
600 g (1 lb 5 oz) cherries, pitted
250 g (9 oz) strawberries, hulled and halved

Combine the orange juice, lemon juice, sugar and vanilla pod in a wide saucepan and bring to a simmer. Add the apricot halves, cover and simmer for 5 minutes. Using a slotted spoon, transfer the apricots to a bowl.

Add the pitted cherries to the syrup and simmer gently for 1 minute. Gently stir in the strawberries and cook for 1 minute, without boiling.

Mix together the cherries, strawberries and syrup with the apricots and stir gently. Set aside to cool, then chill before serving.

Peaches with Raspberry Coulis

SERVES 6–8

When the peaches are perfectly ripe, this fruity dessert tastes absolutely beautiful.
It is best served at room temperature, but should be refrigerated if you are not serving
it within 30 minutes.

250 g (9 oz) raspberries
1 tablespoon caster (superfine) sugar
juice of 2 oranges
juice of ½ lemon
130 g (4½ oz) blueberries
4 ripe peaches
2 tablespoons Drambuie, brandy, Kirsch or
    Cointreau (optional)

In a food processor, blend the raspberries, sugar, orange
and lemon juice to a purée. Pass the purée through a fine
strainer into a serving bowl.

Gently stir the blueberries into the raspberry sauce.

Halve and stone the peaches and cut them into segments
about 2 cm (¾ in) thick, adding them to the raspberry
mixture as you slice them.

Stir in the Drambuie, if using, just before serving.

Mango, Kiwi and Mint Coupe

SERVES 6

This simple refreshing dessert is ideal to round off a rich meal.

juice of 1 orange
juice of 1 lime
1 tablespoon caster (superfine) sugar
6 mint leaves
1 tablespoon Drambuie or brandy (optional)
3 mangoes
3 kiwifruit

Combine the orange and lime juice in a mixing bowl. Stir in the sugar, mint leaves and Drambuie, if using.

Peel the mangoes and kiwifruit. Using a melon baller, scoop out balls of mango and kiwifruit. Gently toss the fruit with the juice mixture, then refrigerate until required.

Spoon the fruit and juice into small glasses or coupes to serve.

Minted Poached Quinces with Cocoa Sauce

SERVES 4

I spent much of my youth playing under a handsome quince tree that produced several hundred kilograms of fruit every year. We made huge quantities of quince jelly, much of which we gave away. Serve this dessert either with cream, ice cream or Crème Anglaise (page 185). You can buy non-alcoholic green peppermint syrup from specialty grocers and some liquor stores.

½ vanilla pod
grated zest of 1 orange
grated zest of 1 lemon
300 g (10½ oz) sugar
3 or 4 quinces, peeled, quartered and cored
60 ml (2 fl oz/¼ cup) green peppermint syrup
½ quantity Cocoa Sauce (page 185)
cream, ice cream or Crème Anglaise (p 185),
    to serve

Place 1 litre (34 fl oz/4 cups) water in a saucepan with the vanilla pod, orange zest, lemon zest and sugar. Bring to the boil, then reduce the heat and simmer for 10 minutes.

Add the quinces to the pan and simmer for 20 minutes. Add the peppermint syrup and simmer for another 2 minutes. Set aside to cool, then refrigerate for 24 hours for the quinces to absorb the flavour of the syrup.

To serve, strain the quinces, discarding the syrup. Spoon 2 tablespoons of the cocoa sauce into the centre of four serving plates and top with the quince quarters. Serve with cream, ice cream or crème anglaise.

Mixed Berries with Kirsch in Tulip Baskets

SERVES 8

The delicate baskets are made using *langues de chat*, 'cat's tongue' biscuits (cookies). To shape the baskets, I use small brioche moulds or the back of a teacup. Raspberries, strawberries and blueberries are lovely but you can also use diced mango mixed with passionfruit or other seasonal fruit.

90 g (3 oz) butter, softened
90 g (3 oz) caster (superfine) sugar
3 large egg whites
90 g (3 oz) plain (all-purpose) flour, sifted
70 g (2½ oz) raspberry jam
2 tablespoons Kirsch or Drambuie
300 g (10½ oz) raspberries
300 g (10½ oz) small strawberries
200 g (7 oz) blueberries
250 ml (8½ fl oz/1 cup) cream, whipped until firm, or 8 scoops Vanilla Ice Cream (page 128 or store-bought) or a fruit sorbet of your choice

Preheat the oven to 180°C (350°F). Line a baking tray with baking paper.

In a small bowl, whisk together the butter and sugar. Mix in the egg whites, and lastly mix in the sifted flour.

Spoon the mixture into a piping bag fitted with a 5 cm (2 in) nozzle and pipe a 10 cm (4 in) ring onto the prepared baking tray, then pipe three or four rings inside the large one. Using a small spatula, flatten the rings to form a thin, flat disc.

In batches, bake the discs for a few minutes or until the edges of the biscuit (cookie) are golden brown and the centre looks dry. Remove from the oven and use a spatula to quickly lift the biscuit off the tray with a scraping movement. Press the warm biscuit into a brioche mould or over the back of a teacup to make a tulip shape. The biscuit will harden as it cools so the shape must be formed while it is still hot. Leave in the mould for a few minutes until cool, then remove and set aside while you prepare the remaining baskets.

Combine the raspberry jam and Kirsch in a bowl. Add the fruit and gently mix together.

Fill each tulip basket with the mixed berries and top with a little cream, ice cream or sorbet. Serve immediately.

Stewed Blueberries with Crème Chiboust

SERVES 6

Stewed blueberries have a lovely intense flavour. The crème chiboust is a light custard set with a little gelatine.

30 g (1 oz) caster (superfine) sugar
juice of 2 lemons
1/4 star anise
600 g (1 lb 5 oz) blueberries

CRÈME CHIBOUST
1 gelatine leaf
250 ml (8 1/2 fl oz/1 cup) milk
2 large eggs, separated
70 g (2 1/2 oz) caster (superfine) sugar
20 g (3/4 oz) plain (all-purpose) flour
1 tablespoon finely grated lemon zest

Combine the sugar with the lemon juice and star anise in a saucepan and bring to a simmer. Stir in the blueberries and cook, stirring gently, for 2 minutes. Transfer the blueberries to a bowl to cool. Discard the star anise.

To make the crème chiboust, place the gelatine leaf in a large bowl, cover with cold water and set aside for about 15 minutes. Meanwhile, heat the milk in a small saucepan.

Combine the egg yolks with 20 g (3/4 oz) of the sugar in a bowl. Stir in the flour and lemon zest. Whisk in the hot milk, then pour the mixture into a saucepan and stir over low heat until the mixture thickens. Transfer to a bowl. Squeeze out any water from the gelatine leaf and whisk the gelatine into the custard. Set aside until cold.

Using electric beaters, beat the egg whites with 25 g (1 oz) of the sugar until very firm and shiny. Beat in the remaining sugar, then gently fold the mixture into the cold custard. Spoon the crème chiboust into a piping bag.

Spoon some of the cold blueberries and juice into six whisky glasses or other small glasses. Pipe a 3 cm (1 in) layer of crème chiboust over the berries, then add a little more berries and juice. Cover with plastic wrap and refrigerate for 2–3 hours before serving.

Tropical Fruit Salad

SERVES 6

I've made this beautiful tropical fruit salad several times when cooking for French visitors. It is very refreshing at the end of a summer barbecue. It can be served with vanilla ice cream or a fruit sorbet.

juice of 1 orange
pulp of 3 passionfruit
1 tablespoon caster (superfine) sugar
1 mango
⅓ pineapple
½ pink papaya
12 fresh or canned lychees

Combine the orange juice, passionfruit pulp and sugar in a bowl.

Peel the mango and pineapple, cut them into bite-sized pieces and add to the bowl. Peel the papaya and remove the seeds. Cut the papaya into cubes or scoop into balls, and add to the bowl. Peel the lychees and add them to the bowl. Gently toss the fruits together and serve.

Caramelised Red Plums with Berries

SERVES 6

This is a truly luscious dish with a magnificent ruby-red colour. Dust it with icing sugar just before serving for a beautiful presentation.

seeds of ½ vanilla pod
80 g (3 oz/⅓ cup) caster (superfine) sugar
200 g (7 oz) raspberries
200 g (7 oz) blueberries
juice of 1 orange
juice of ½ lemon
6–12 red plums, halved and stoned
200 g (7 oz) blackberries
icing (confectioners') sugar, for dusting

Mix the vanilla seeds with the sugar.

In a food processor, blend half of the raspberries, one-third of the blueberries, the orange juice, lemon juice and half of the vanilla sugar to a purée. Strain this sauce into a jug.

Place the plums, cut-side up, in a gratin dish. Sprinkle the remaining sugar over the plums and place under a hot grill (broiler) until the sugar starts to bubble.

Pour a little berry sauce in the centre of six serving plates. Place the plum halves on the sauce and arrange the blackberries and remaining raspberries and blueberries around the plums. Dust with a little icing sugar and serve.

Apple and Quince Terrine with Raspberry and Vanilla Sauce

SERVES 8–10

During my childhood in the Loire Valley, my grandmother often served apples and quinces together for an exotic flavour. Set in a terrine, it's a superb combination.

1 kg (2 lb 3 oz) cameo or Golden Delicious
   apples
1 quince
375 ml (13 fl oz/1½ cups) fresh orange juice
zest of ½ lemon
80 g (3 oz/⅓ cup) caster (superfine) sugar
½ vanilla pod, split lengthwise
10 g (½ oz) powdered gelatine
whipped cream, to serve
1 quantity Raspberry and Vanilla Sauce
   (page 187)

Peel, core and quarter the apples and quince. Cut the quince quarters into long, thin slices. Cut the apple quarters in half.

Combine the orange juice, lemon zest, sugar and vanilla pod in a saucepan. Add the apple and quince pieces and bring to a simmer. Cover and cook, stirring occasionally, for 15 minutes or until the apple and quince are soft. Remove the vanilla pod.

Strain the cooking liquid into a bowl and stir in the gelatine until dissolved. Return the liquid to the pan with the fruit and stir well.

Spoon the fruit and liquid into a 25 x 11 cm (10 x 4½ in) loaf (bar) tin or terrine mould lined with plastic wrap, then refrigerate for 2–3 hours to set.

Dip the terrine mould in hot water for 20 seconds, then turn out onto a serving platter. Cut into slices and serve with whipped cream and the raspberry and vanilla sauce.

Roast Peaches with Fruit Salsa

SERVES 4

This is a summer treat to make when peaches are at their best. If you wish, replace the peaches with apricots, the strawberries with raspberries and the Kirsch with Drambuie.

1 banana
6 large strawberries
$\frac{1}{4}$ pineapple, peeled and cored
juice of 1 orange
1 tablespoon finely grated lemon zest
80 g (3 oz/$\frac{1}{3}$ cup) caster (superfine) sugar
40 g (1$\frac{1}{2}$ oz) brown sugar
4 soft, ripe peaches, halved and stoned
30 g (1 oz) butter, chopped
60 ml (2 fl oz/$\frac{1}{4}$ cup) Kirsch

Preheat the oven to 200°C (400°F). Butter an oval ovenproof dish that is large enough to hold the eight peach halves.

Dice the banana, strawberries and pineapple and combine with the orange juice, lemon zest, half the caster sugar and half the brown sugar.

Add the diced fruit to the prepared dish. Place the peaches, skin-side down, on top of the diced fruit. Sprinkle with the remaining brown sugar and caster sugar and dot with small knobs of butter.

Bake for 20 minutes or until the peaches are cooked.

Bring the Kirsch to the boil in a small saucepan. Pour the hot Kirsch over the hot peaches and light with a match. The Kirsch and peaches must be very hot for the Kirsch to ignite. Serve immediately.

Blood Orange, Mango and Pineapple Salad

SERVES 4

When the fruits are perfectly ripe, this simple fruit salad is stunning. You can vary the fruits to suit your taste. It looks beautiful in whisky glasses.

juice of 4 blood oranges
juice of ½ lemon
1 tablespoon sugar
1 banana, cut into 5 mm (¼ in) slices
1 large mango, peeled and diced
⅓ pineapple, diced
2 golden kiwifruit, diced
pulp of 2 passionfruit

Combine the orange juice, lemon juice and sugar in a bowl. Add the banana, mango, pineapple and kiwifruit.

Stir in the passionfruit pulp and serve immediately. Alternatively, cover and refrigerate until 15 minutes before serving.

Poached Apricots and Peaches with Toasted Almonds

SERVES 6

You can serve this simple, light summer dessert with whipped cream, ice cream or custard, or use as the filling for a tart.

juice of 2 lemons

100 g (3½ oz) sugar

½ vanilla pod, split lengthwise

12 ripe apricots, halved and stoned

3 ripe peaches, halved and stoned

1 tablespoon cognac, Armagnac or Drambuie (optional)

200 ml (7 fl oz) cream, whipped until firm

120 g (4 oz/1⅓ cup) flaked almonds, toasted

6 scoops Vanilla Ice Cream (page 128 or store-bought)

icing (confectioners') sugar, for dusting

Combine 100 ml (3½ fl oz) water, the lemon juice, sugar and vanilla pod in a wide saucepan and bring to the boil.

Place the apricots and peaches in the syrup and shake the pan so the fruit is well coated. Cover the pan with baking paper or foil and simmer for 15 minutes or until the fruit is soft. Transfer the fruit to a bowl and stir in the cognac, if using. Set aside to cool, then refrigerate until cold.

Spoon the cream into a piping bag fitted with a small serrated nozzle. Pipe a little cream into six tall glasses. Top with the poached apricots and peaches and sprinkle half the almonds on top. Add a scoop of vanilla ice cream and pipe rosettes of whipped cream on top. Sprinkle the remaining toasted almonds on top and dust with icing sugar before serving.

Blood Orange, Mango and Pineapple Salad

Poached Apricots and Peaches
with Toasted Almonds

Pineapple and Raspberries with Crème Fraîche Chantilly

SERVES 4

Choose a very ripe and sweet pineapple and the best raspberries for this dessert.
If the raspberries are not sweet, use strawberries or blackberries.

juice of 1 lemon
55 g (2½ oz/¼ cup) sugar
seeds of ½ vanilla pod
8 round slices of fresh pineapple, about 5 mm
    (¼ in) thick
200 ml (7 fl oz) crème fraîche or cream
    (40% fat)
2 teaspoons milk
400 g (14 oz) raspberries

Combine the lemon juice, 2½ tablespoons water and 40 g (2 oz) of the sugar in a small saucepan. Bring to a simmer and cook for 1 minute. Transfer the syrup to a heatproof bowl. Stir in the vanilla seeds and set aside to cool.

Trim off the pineapple skin and cut out the hard centre core from each slice.

Place half the lemon syrup in a small tray and top with the pineapple slices, taking care not to break them. Pour the remaining syrup over the top, cover with plastic wrap and refrigerate for at least 1 hour.

Using electric beaters, beat the crème fraîche and milk in a bowl until almost firm. Beat in the remaining sugar. Refrigerate until required.

Place a pineapple ring on each plate and top with the raspberries. Add a second pineapple ring and spoon some of the syrup over the top.

Pipe or spoon a little of the crème fraîche mixture into the centre of each pineapple ring and serve immediately.

sorbets and ice creams

Strawberry Vacherin with Mango and Raspberries

SERVES 8–10

Make sure you mould the vanilla ice cream and strawberry sorbet at least 1 hour before serving. You can make the meringues the day before.

½ quantity Vanilla Ice Cream (page 128)
1 quantity Strawberry Sorbet with Vanilla
　　(page 129)
200 ml (7 fl oz) cream, whipped until firm
1 quantity Meringues (page 182)
200 g (7 oz) raspberries
1 large mango, peeled and chopped
pulp of 1 passionfruit

Place a 2 litre (68 fl oz) charlotte mould in the freezer to chill.

Mould the vanilla ice cream in the charlotte mould and top with the strawberry sorbet. Place in the freezer for at least 1 hour to set well.

Dip the mould in warm water and carefully unmould the ice cream onto a serving dish. Use a little whipped cream to attach the meringues around the side of the ice cream. You may need to trim a few meringues with a knife to fit neatly, and you may not use them all. If you wish, use a piping bag fitted with a fluted nozzle to pipe cream into the spaces in between the meringues.

Top the dessert with the raspberries, mango pieces and passionfruit pulp. Serve by carefully cutting the vacherin into wedges, cutting in between the meringues.

Coffee and Grand Marnier Parfait with Walnuts

SERVES 6–8

You don't need an ice cream maker for this delicious ice cream, but allow 8 hours for freezing, and turn the freezer to the coldest setting a couple of hours beforehand. When the parfait is firm, return the temperature setting to normal.

40 g (1½ oz/⅓ cup) sultanas (golden raisins)
2 tablespoons Grand Marnier
6 large egg yolks
175 g (6 oz) sugar
2 teaspoons instant coffee powder
2 tablespoons milk
60 g (2 oz/½ cup) walnuts, chopped, plus
    extra, to serve
310 ml (10 fl oz/1¼ cups) cream, whipped
    until firm

Place the sultanas and Grand Marnier in a bowl, cover and microwave on high for 20 seconds.

Place the egg yolks in a mixing bowl.

Combine the sugar and 125 ml (4 fl oz/½ cup) water in a saucepan and bring to the boil. Cook for 8 minutes or until the colour turns slightly yellow. When the syrup is ready, a teaspoon of the syrup dipped into cold water will solidify.

Use electric beaters to beat the egg yolks on high speed. Slowly pour the syrup onto the yolks and continue beating until the mixture is white and fluffy and has cooled. This will take at least 6–7 minutes. If some of the syrup solidifies in the mixture, continue beating as the heat of the mixture should melt it.

Dissolve the coffee in the milk, then stir it into the sultana mixture. Mix in the egg-yolk mixture, then add the walnuts.

Gently fold the cream into the mixture. Pour into a 2 litre (68 fl oz) mould and freeze for at least 8 hours.

To serve, scoop the parfait from the mould or unmould it by briefly dipping the mould in hot water and inverting it onto a plate. It can be unmoulded ahead of time and kept in the freezer until required. Serve sprinkled with the extra chopped walnuts.

Christmas Ice Cream Cake

SERVES 8–10

The combination of raisins, sultanas (golden raisins) and glacé (candied) cherries with the rum in this lovely frozen ice cream makes a refreshing change from the traditional hot Christmas pudding. You can mould it in a pudding basin, a cake tin or even in individual glasses. As this pudding is rich, you only need a small serve.

2 tablespoons sultanas (golden raisins)
2 tablespoons raisins
2 tablespoons currants
6 green glacé (candied) cherries, diced
6 red glacé (candied) cherries, diced
60 ml (2 fl oz/¼ cup) rum or brandy
6 large egg yolks
230 g (8 oz/1 cup) caster (superfine) sugar
300 ml (10 fl oz) cream, whipped until firm
mixed berries, to serve
1 quantity Raspberry Coulis (page 189),
    to serve

Place the sultanas, raisins, currants and glacé cherries in a small bowl. Pour in the rum, mix well and leave to macerate for at least 4 hours, stirring two or three times.

Place the egg yolks in a mixing bowl.

Combine the sugar and 125 ml (4 fl oz/½ cup) water in a saucepan and bring to the boil. Cook for 8 minutes or until the colour turns slightly yellow. When the syrup is ready, a teaspoon of the syrup dipped into cold water will solidify.

Use electric beaters to beat the egg yolks on high speed. Slowly pour the syrup onto the yolks and continue beating until the mixture is white and fluffy and has cooled. This will take at least 6–7 minutes. If some of the syrup solidifies in the mixture, continue beating as the heat of the mixture should melt it.

Stir in the soaked fruits, then fold in the whipped cream. Pour the mixture into one large mould or into individual moulds and freeze for at least 6 hours before serving with mixed berries and a little raspberry coulis.

Raspberry Sorbet in a Fruit Coupe

SERVES 6

Raspberry is one of my favourite sorbet flavours, especially when raspberries are at their sweetest. I've suggested a range of fruits but use what's best in season.

750 g (1 lb 10 oz) raspberries
330 g (11 oz/1½ cups) sugar
juice of 2 oranges
juice of 1½ lemons
1 large mango
pulp of 3 passionfruit
200 g (7 oz) blueberries
1 tablespoon caster (superfine) sugar
whipped cream, to serve

Place a 2 litre (68 fl oz) mould in the freezer to chill for 1 hour.

In a food processor, blend two-thirds of the raspberries to a purée with the sugar, orange juice and the juice of one lemon. Strain the purée, discarding the raspberry seeds.

Pour the raspberry purée into an ice cream maker and churn until firm. Transfer the sorbet to the chilled mould and place in the freezer.

Peel the mango, cut into cubes, and place in a bowl with the passionfruit pulp, blueberries, remaining raspberries, caster sugar and remaining lemon juice.

Spoon a little of the fruit into six glasses or coupes and top with a scoop or two of raspberry sorbet. Serve the whipped cream separately or pipe it decoratively around the sorbet.

Chocolate and Cointreau Ice Cream with Glacé Orange

SERVES 8

This is a great dessert to finish a festive meal, and one I tend to serve in winter when there are not as many fresh fruits around.

5 large egg yolks
145 g (5 oz/⅔ cup) caster (superfine) sugar
500 ml (17 fl oz/2 cups) milk
120 g (4 oz) dark chocolate, chopped
5 slices of glacé (candied) orange
375 ml (13 fl oz/1½ cups) cream, whipped until firm
1½ tablespoons Cointreau

Place a 2 litre (68 fl oz) mould in the freezer to chill.

Using electric beaters, beat the egg yolks and sugar in a large heatproof bowl until the mixture forms a ribbon.

Meanwhile, bring the milk to the boil in a saucepan. Pour the hot milk onto the egg-yolk mixture and whisk well. Return the mixture to the pan and, using a wooden spatula, stir over medium heat until the custard thickens slightly and lightly coats the back of the spoon. Don't allow the custard to boil as it will curdle. Remove from the heat, strain into a bowl and whisk in the chocolate until melted. Set aside to cool.

Dice two of the glacé orange slices and cut the other three in half.

Stir the whipped cream into the chocolate mixture and pour the mixture into an ice cream maker. Churn until the ice cream is quite firm. Add the Cointreau and churn until firm.

Transfer the ice cream to the chilled mould, sprinkling in the diced glacé orange pieces as you fill the mould. Place the ice cream in the freezer to set for at least 3–4 hours.

Carefully unmould the ice cream onto a dish or scoop it into glasses. Garnish with the glacé orange halves.

Plombières Ice Cream Cake

SERVES 6–8

Plombières ice cream is flavoured with almonds and glacé (candied) fruits steeped in Kirsch, and it's a great dinner party dessert. For a special effect, use a cake tin with an unusual shape.

50 g (2 oz) mixed diced glacé
  (candied) fruit
1½ tablespoons Kirsch
500 ml (17 fl oz/2 cups) milk
½ vanilla pod, split lengthwise
55 g (2 oz/½ cup) ground almonds
4 egg yolks
145 g (5 oz/⅔ cup) caster (superfine) sugar
250 ml (8½ fl oz/1 cup) cream, whipped
  until firm
600 g (1 lb 5 oz) seasonal fruit, to serve
icing (confectioners') sugar, for dusting
1 quantity Raspberry and Vanilla Sauce
  (page 187), to serve

Place a 25 x 11 cm (10 x 4½ in) loaf (bar) tin or 20–25 cm (8–10 in) cake tin in the freezer to chill.

Combine the glacé fruits with the Kirsch and set aside.

Heat the milk, vanilla pod and ground almonds in a large saucepan.

Using electric beaters, beat the egg yolks and sugar in a heatproof bowl for about 5 minutes or until light and fluffy. Pour the hot milk onto the egg mixture, whisking quickly to prevent the eggs from scrambling. Return the mixture to the saucepan and cook over medium heat, stirring constantly, making a figure eight with a wooden spatula, until the mixture coats the back of the spatula. Strain the custard into a heatproof bowl and discard the ground almonds and vanilla pod. Whisk for a few seconds to help the custard to cool.

Transfer the custard to an ice cream maker and churn until firm. Add the glacé fruits and churn a little more before adding the whipped cream. Churn again until well incorporated. Place in the chilled mould, cover with baking paper and freeze for at least 2 hours before serving.

Unmould the ice cream onto a chilled dish. Serve the ice cream with fruit, dusted with a little icing sugar, and the sauce on the side.

Chocolate and Cointreau Ice Cream with Glacé Orange

Plombières Ice Cream Cake

Frozen Chococcino Soufflés

SERVES 6

It is best to prepare these frozen soufflés 4–6 hours before required. Make them in your most attractive small coffee cups.

250 ml (8½ fl oz/1 cup) milk
½ vanilla pod, split lengthwise
2 egg yolks
55 g (2 oz/¼ cup) caster (superfinc) sugar
25 g (1 oz) plain (all-purpose) flour, sifted
60 g (2 oz) dark chocolate, chopped
250 ml (8½ fl oz/1 cup) cream, whipped until firm
3 egg whites
pinch of cream of tartar
50 g (2 oz) icing (confectioners') sugar, plus extra, for dusting
Dutch (unsweetened) cocoa powder, for dusting

Fit six small coffee cups with collars made from a double layer of baking paper, extending about 3 cm (1 in) above the rims of the cups. Use string to hold the collars in place.

Combine the milk and vanilla pod in a small saucepan and bring to the boil.

Using electric beaters, beat the egg yolks and caster sugar in a heatproof bowl for about 2 minutes. Stir in the sifted flour until just combined. Pour the hot milk onto the mixture and whisk until combined. Return the mixture to the saucepan and cook over medium heat, whisking constantly, for 1–2 minutes or until thickened. Transfer to a bowl and whisk in the chocolate. Discard the vanilla pod and set aside to cool.

Fold the whipped cream into the cold custard.

Using electric beaters, beat the egg whites and cream of tartar until slightly stiff. Add the icing sugar and beat until stiff peaks form. Gently fold into the custard.

Spoon the mixture into the prepared cups to about 2 cm (³⁄₄ in) above the rims. Place the soufflés in the freezer to set for about 4–6 hours.

Remove the soufflés from the freezer 5 minutes before serving. Dust with cocoa powder and icing sugar, carefully remove the paper collars and serve immediately.

Pineapple and Coconut Ice Cream with Seasonal Fruits

SERVES 6–8

This ice cream is very refreshing at the end of a special meal or you can just serve it as an afternoon treat. The pineapple needs to be perfectly ripe.

1 pineapple
230 g (8 oz/1 cup) caster (superfine) sugar
juice of 2 oranges
juice of 1 lemon
45 g (2 oz/½ cup) desiccated (shredded) coconut plus 1 tablespoon extra, for garnishing
250 ml (8½ fl oz/1 cup) cream, whipped until firm
sliced fruit, such as peach, nectarine, mango and pineapple, to serve
mint leaves, for garnishing

Peel and trim the pineapple. Cut it into quarters and remove the hard centre core. Cut the flesh into cubes.

In a food processor, blend the pineapple, sugar, orange juice, lemon juice and coconut to a purée.

Transfer the mixture to an ice cream maker. Churn until the mixture begins to harden, then add the whipped cream and churn until the ice cream is firm. Transfer to a container, cover and store in the freezer.

If you don't have an ice cream maker, place the pineapple mixture in a metal bowl in the freezer. When it has hardened a little, remove from the freezer and whisk in the whipped cream. Return to the freezer until it has hardened slightly, then whisk again. Repeat this once or twice until the mixture is too hard to whisk. Store in a covered container in the freezer.

Place some fruit slices in a chilled coupe. Top with several balls of pineapple ice cream, sprinkle with coconut and serve garnished with a few mint leaves.

Frozen Apricot Soufflé with Hazelnut Praline

SERVES 6

Finish off a special dinner with this frozen dessert. It's made with softened dried apricots, and there is no last-minute preparation.

18 dried apricots
juice of ½ lemon
1 quantity Crème Pâtissière (page 184)
185 ml (6 fl oz/¾ cup) cream, whipped
    until firm
4 large egg whites
pinch of cream of tartar
55 g (2 oz/¼ cup) caster (superfine) sugar
1 quantity Hazelnut Praline (page 184)

Fit six individual soufflé moulds with baking paper collars, extending about 3 cm (1 in) above the rims of the moulds. Use string to hold the collars in place.

Place the dried apricots in a saucepan, cover with cold water and bring to the boil. Turn off the heat, cover with a lid and set aside for 10 minutes. Drain the apricots and blend in a food processor to a fine purée. Set the purée over a bowl of ice to cool.

Combine the apricot purée with the lemon juice and crème pâtissière, then gently stir in the whipped cream.

Using electric beaters, beat the egg whites and cream of tartar until slightly stiff. Add the sugar and beat until stiff peaks form. Gently fold into the apricot cream. Spoon the mixture into a piping bag without a nozzle.

Spoon a third of the hazelnut praline into the bottom of the soufflé moulds. Pipe half of the apricot mixture on top, then add another third of the praline. Fill with the remaining apricot mixture to about 2 cm (¾ in) above the rim.

Place the soufflés in the freezer to set for about 6 hours.

Sprinkle the remaining praline on top of the frozen soufflés, carefully remove the paper collars and serve immediately.

hot desserts

Grand Marnier Soufflés

SERVES 6

This very classic French dessert is fun to make, but it also requires a little care. A soufflé contains eggs, and when eggs are cooked they become firm, so a well-cooked soufflé is firm, too, but only for a short time. Don't be in too much of a hurry to remove your soufflé from the oven — if it falls, it is not cooked enough.

60 ml (2 fl oz/¼ cup) Grand Marnier
310 ml (10 fl oz/1¼ cups) Crème Pâtissière (page 184), chilled
6 large egg whites
pinch of cream of tartar
1 tablespoon caster (superfine) sugar
icing (confectioners') sugar, for dusting

Preheat the oven to 150°C (300°F). Butter six 185 ml (6 fl oz/¾ cup) soufflé moulds and dust with caster (superfine) sugar.

Whisk the Grand Marnier into the crème pâtissière.

Using electric beaters, beat the egg whites and cream of tartar until almost stiff. Add the sugar and beat until firm. Using a large metal spoon or rubber spatula, mix a little of the egg white into the crème pâtissière, then gently fold in the remaining egg white.

Spoon the mixture into the prepared moulds and smooth the tops with a spatula. The mixture should not touch the rim of the moulds.

Bake for 5 minutes, then increase the temperature to 205°C (400°F). Bake for a further 5 minutes, then increase the temperature to 230°C (450°F) and bake for a further 5 minutes.

Remove the soufflés from the oven, dust with a little icing sugar and serve immediately. If a short delay is unavoidable, leave in the oven at the lowest possible temperature for a few more minutes.

Peach Crumble

SERVES 6

I love baked peaches and this crumble is really special. Make sure the peaches are ripe and juicy.

CRUMBLE
60 g (2 oz) chilled butter, cubed
55 g (2 oz/¼ cup) caster (superfine) sugar
pinch of salt
60 g (2 oz) plain (all-purpose) flour, sifted
60 g (2 oz) ground almonds

6 ripe peaches, halved and stoned
30 g (1 oz) butter
30 g (1 oz) caster (superfine) sugar
2 tablespoons lemon zest
juice of half an orange

Place the crumble ingredients in a bowl and mix with a wooden spoon or the tips of your fingers until the mixture forms a crumbly dough. Place on a plate and refrigerate while you prepare the peaches.

Preheat the oven to 180°C (350°F).

Cut each peach half into three segments. Melt the butter in a large frying pan. Add the sugar and lemon zest and bring to the boil. Add the peach segments and toss gently for 2 minutes. Stir in the orange juice. Transfer the peaches to a bowl.

Pour the cooking liquid into a 25–28 cm (10–11 in) square ovenproof dish and arrange the peach segments on top. Sprinkle the crumble dough over the peaches.

Bake for 20–25 minutes or until the topping is golden.

Self-Saucing Chocolate Pudding

SERVES 6

This pudding reminds me of a rich soufflé and it's so easy to make. It's definitely one for chocolate lovers.

150 g (5 oz/1 cup) self-raising flour
40 g (1½ oz/⅓ cup) dark Dutch (unsweetened) cocoa powder
60 g (2 oz) butter, softened
115 g (4 oz/½ cup) caster (superfine) sugar
1 tablespoon finely grated orange zest
1 large egg, beaten
60 g (2 oz/½ cup) walnuts, coarsely chopped
125 ml (4 fl oz/½ cup) milk
95 g (3½ oz/½ cup) brown sugar
icing (confectioners') sugar, for dusting
ice cream or cream, to serve

Preheat the oven to 190°C (375°F). Butter a deep 25 cm (10 in) ceramic or metal pie dish or 6 individual 250 ml (8½ fl oz/1 cup) ramekin dishes.

Sift the flour and half of the cocoa powder together. Using a whisk, beat the butter, caster sugar and orange zest in a bowl until creamy. Add the egg and walnuts and mix well. Stir in the sifted flour mixture and the milk. Pour the mixture into the prepared dish.

Combine the brown sugar and remaining cocoa powder and sprinkle over the batter. Gently pour 500 ml (17 fl oz/2 cups) boiling water over the top. Bake for 45 minutes for a large pudding or 25 minutes for individual puddings, until the top is firm and you can see the sauce around the side of the dish. Lightly dust the pudding with icing sugar and serve with ice cream or cream.

Flamed Bananas with Rum

SERVES 6

Take care when adding the rum to the pan and igniting it. If you are serving this to children, you can omit the rum and the flaming of the bananas.

6 ripe bananas
115 g (4 oz/½ cup) caster (superfine) sugar
50 g (2 oz) butter
60 ml (2 fl oz/¼ cup) rum
100 ml (3½ fl oz) cream
6 scoops Vanilla Ice Cream (page 128 or store-bought)

Peel the bananas and liberally coat them with the sugar.

Melt the butter in a non-stick frying pan over medium heat. Add the bananas and excess sugar and cook for a few minutes on each side until the sugar caramelises and turns golden brown.

Slowly pour the rum into the pan, then very carefully light a match and ignite the rum. Shake the pan a little to prevent the bananas from sticking.

When the flame is out, pour in the cream and boil for a few seconds.

Transfer the bananas to serving plates, spooning a little sauce over them. Serve with a scoop of vanilla ice cream.

Self-Saucing Chocolate Pudding

Flamed Bananas with Rum

Christmas Pudding

MAKES 1 LARGE OR 2 SMALLER PUDDINGS

This recipe will make two puddings or one very large one, and will serve about twenty people. I like to prepare my pudding at least two or three weeks before Christmas.

250 g (9 oz) butter, softened
250 g (9 oz) brown sugar
1 teaspoon grated lemon zest
1 teaspoon grated orange zest
4 large eggs
125 g (4 oz/1 cup) raisins
250 g (9 oz/2 cups) sultanas (golden raisins)
250 g (9 oz/1⅔ cups) currants
125 g (4 oz/⅔ cup) shredded mixed peel
1 small apple, grated
1 carrot, grated
100 g (3½ oz/⅔ cup) self-raising flour, sifted
100 g (3½ oz/⅔ cup) plain (all-purpose) flour, sifted, plus extra, for dusting
1 teaspoon ground nutmeg
1 teaspoon mixed spice
½ teaspoon bicarbonate of soda (baking soda)
125 g (4 oz) fresh or dried breadcrumbs
60 g (2 oz/½ cup) slivered blanched almonds
80 ml (3 fl oz/⅓ cup) brandy
cream, ice cream or custard, to serve

Cream the butter and sugar with the lemon and orange zest. Add the eggs one at a time, mixing well after each one. Mix in the dried fruits, mixed peel, apple and carrot. Sift together the flours, nutmeg, mixed spice and bicarbonate of soda and add this to the mixture. Add in the breadcrumbs and almonds and stir in the brandy. Set aside for about 30 minutes.

Drop a 70 cm (27½ in) square of calico or two 60 cm (24 in) squares of calico into a saucepan of boiling water and boil for 3 minutes, then rinse and boil again. Remove from the water, wring out and lay flat. Sprinkle the extra flour into the centre of the calico to form a layer about 1 mm (¹⁄₁₆ in) thick, leaving a border of about 20 cm (8 in) all around the edge.

Spoon the pudding mixture into the centre of the cloth. Close the cloth around the pudding mixture and tie firmly with kitchen string, leaving a 5 cm (2 in) gap at the top to allow for expansion during cooking. Leave enough string to hang the pudding when it is cooked.

Cook, covered in simmering water for 4 hours for two smaller puddings or 7 hours for a large pudding, topping up with boiling water as required to keep the pudding covered. Remove the pudding from the water and hang it in a dry place with good air circulation for quick drying.

On Christmas day, reheat the pudding by simmering in water for 2 hours. Serve with cream, ice cream or custard.

Rhubarb and Apple Crumble

SERVES 6

We love this crumble at our house. You can use other fruits, such as apricots, peaches or prunes, or you could add a few berries. It's not as rich as a traditional butter crumble.

8 rhubarb stalks, peeled and diced
2 Golden Delicious or Granny Smith apples,
　　peeled, cored and diced
1 tablespoon grated orange zest
2 tablespoons caster (superfine) sugar
65 g (2 oz/⅔ cup) rolled oats
1 tablespoon wholemeal (whole-wheat) plain
　　(all-purpose) flour
1 tablespoon desiccated (shredded) coconut
2 tablespoons chopped raw almonds
1 tablespoon butter or olive oil
1 tablespoon honey
cream or ice cream, to serve

Preheat the oven to 210°C (410°F).

Place the rhubarb, apple, orange zest and 2 tablespoons water in a large saucepan. Cook over medium heat for 10 minutes or until the apple and rhubarb are just soft. Stir in the sugar. Spoon the mixture into a 25–28 cm (10–11 in) gratin dish.

Using your hands, thoroughly combine the rolled oats, flour, coconut, almonds, butter and honey in a bowl.

Spread the crumble mixture over the apple and rhubarb and pat down slightly. Bake for 10–15 minutes or until the top is golden brown.

Serve hot or cold with cream or ice cream.

Nectarine Gratin

SERVES 4

We had a nectarine tree in our small vineyard in France, and I adore nectarines. Buy them regularly during the summer and you'll learn how to recognise when they are ripe.

6 white or yellow nectarines, halved and
    stoned
2 tablespoons orange juice
2 tablespoons brown sugar
1 tablespoon caster (superfine) sugar
2 egg yolks
1 tablespoon brandy
1 tablespoon finely grated lemon zest
250 ml (9 fl oz/1 cup) cream, whipped
    until firm

Preheat the oven to 200°C (400°F). Butter a gratin dish large enough to hold twelve nectarine halves.

Place the nectarines, cut side up, in the gratin dish. Pour the orange juice into the dish and sprinkle the brown sugar and caster sugar over the nectarines. Bake for 20 minutes or until the nectarines are soft but not mushy. (This step can be done in advance.)

Place the egg yolks in a small glass bowl and whisk in the brandy and lemon zest. Place the bowl over a saucepan of hot water over low heat. Whisk the yolks for 5 minutes or until light and fluffy. They must stay creamy but not scramble. Remove the bowl from the heat and fold in the whipped cream.

Pour the cream mixture over the cooked nectarines. Cook under a medium grill (broiler) for 2–3 minutes or until slightly browned. Serve immediately.

Lemon Delicious

Kiwi, Banana and Strawberry Gratin

SERVES 4–6

Use any fruit of your choosing in this wonderful, inexpensive treat for the family. Perfectly ripe fruit will produce the best results.

6 kiwifruit
2 bananas
200 g (7 oz) strawberries
4 egg yolks
pulp of 2 passionfruit
100 g (3½ oz) caster (superfine) sugar
125 ml (4 fl oz/½ cup) thick (double/heavy)
    cream, whipped until firm

Peel and cut the kiwifruit and bananas into bite-sized pieces. Place in a 25 x 20 cm (10 x 8 in) gratin dish. Hull the strawberries, cutting any large ones in half, and add to the dish.

Combine the egg yolks, passionfruit pulp and sugar in a heatproof bowl. Place the bowl over a saucepan of simmering water and whisk until light and fluffy. This is called a 'sabayon'. Remove from the heat and set aside to cool a little.

Fold the whipped cream into the sabayon, then spread on top of the fruit.

Place the gratin dish under a hot grill (broiler) for a few minutes or until the top is golden brown. Serve immediately.

Mandarin Soufflés

SERVES 6

A good soufflé is something special. It's not an expensive dessert, so try to practise it a couple of times before a special occasion.

6 mandarins
grated zest of 1 mandarin
juice of 1 lemon
grated zest of ½ lemon
75 g (2½ oz/⅓ cup) sugar
2 tablespoons mandarin liqueur, Cointreau,
    Grand Marnier or cognac
2 large egg yolks
4 large egg whites
pinch of cream of tartar
icing (confectioners') sugar, for dusting

Preheat the oven to 180°C (350°F). Butter six 125 ml (4 fl oz/½ cup) soufflé moulds and dust with caster (superfine) sugar.

Peel the mandarins and place the segments in a food processor. Blend for a few seconds then strain the juice, discarding the pulp and seeds.

Place the mandarin juice and zest, lemon juice and zest, 3 tablespoons of the sugar and the liqueur in a small saucepan and cook until syrupy and reduced to about 125 ml (4 fl oz/½ cup). Transfer to a mixing bowl and vigorously whisk in the egg yolks for 2–3 minutes or until the mixture is fluffy and thickened.

Beat the egg whites and cream of tartar until stiff peaks form. Beat the remaining 1 tablespoon sugar into the beaten whites. Using a rubber spatula, stir a little of the egg white into the mandarin mixture, then gently fold in the remaining egg white.

Spoon the mixture into the prepared moulds and smooth the tops with a spatula or knife. Place the soufflés on a baking tray and bake for 5 minutes, then increase the temperature to 200°C (400°F) and bake for a further 5–10 minutes.

Remove the soufflés from the oven, dust with a little icing sugar and serve immediately.

Crêpes with Raspberries and Marmalade

MAKES 12–18

Everyone loves crêpes. At their best they are very thin, and delicious when filled with fresh fruits and cream. You can, of course, replace the raspberries with other berries.

300 g (10½ oz/2 cups) plain (all-purpose) flour, sifted
pinch of salt
1 teaspoon caster (superfine) sugar
2 eggs
500 ml (17 fl oz/2 cups) milk
1 teaspoon oil
1 tablespoon butter
100 g (3½ oz/⅓ cup) orange marmalade
200 ml (7 fl oz) cream (40% fat)
500 g (1 lb 2 oz) raspberries
icing (confectioners') sugar, for dusting

Combine the sifted flour, salt and sugar in a mixing bowl. Make a well in the centre and pour the eggs and half of the milk into the well. Using a whisk, first mix the eggs and milk together, then gradually incorporate the flour, slowly adding the rest of the milk to form a smooth, thin mixture. Strain the mixture through a fine strainer and refrigerate for at least 20 minutes or until required. (If you are in a great rush, you can use it immediately, but the crêpes will not be as smooth.)

Heat the oil and butter in a crêpe pan or other small frying pan until light golden, then whisk into the crêpe batter.

Place the pan over high heat. Pour enough of the crêpe mixture into the hot pan to cover the base of the pan. Twirl the pan in a smooth motion to form a thin, even crêpe. When the top of the crêpe starts to become dry and the base is golden brown, pick it up with a spatula and quickly turn it over. When the base is cooked, transfer the crêpe to a plate. Repeat with the remaining mixture, without adding any more butter or oil to the pan. If the crêpes begin to stick, wipe the pan with absorbent paper and melt a little butter in the pan before cooking the next one.

Spread each crêpe with a little marmalade and cream. Top with a few raspberries, fold over and serve, dusted with icing sugar.

Pineapple Gratin

SERVES 8

When I first tasted pineapple as a young boy, I thought it was the most amazing fruit in the world. I still think it's one of the greatest fruits and this gratin brings out its best flavour.

1 sweet pineapple
2 tablespoons Kirsch
2 tablespoons caster (superfine) sugar
3 oranges
2 egg yolks
1 teaspoon butter
125 ml (4 fl oz/½ cup) cream, whipped
    until firm
32 raspberries
icing (confectioners') sugar, for dusting

Peel and trim the pineapple. Cut it into quarters and remove the hard core. Cut the flesh into small triangles and place in a bowl. Mix in the Kirsch and half the sugar.

Using a sharp knife, peel the oranges, removing all the white pith. Cut the oranges into 1 cm (½ in) slices and place in a 25–28 cm (10–11 in) gratin dish or eight individual gratin dishes.

Place the egg yolks, remaining sugar and the liquid from the pineapple in a mixing bowl and place over a saucepan of simmering water. Beat with a whisk or electric beaters for about 5 minutes or until the mixture is foamy and thickened. It should not stick to the bowl or look like scrambled eggs. Remove the bowl from the heat and set aside to cool.

Melt the butter in a pan and gently heat the pineapple.

Add the whipped cream to the sabayon. Place the warm pineapple pieces on top of the orange pieces in the gratin dish, sprinkle with the raspberries and spoon the sabayon over the fruit.

Cook the gratin under a hot grill (broiler) for 2–3 minutes or until lightly browned. Serve immediately, dusted with a little icing sugar.

basics

Choux Pastry

MAKES 30 SMALL CHOUX PUFFS, 10–12 LARGE CHOUX PUFFS OR 10 PARIS BREST

This is the very first pastry I learned to make as a sixteen-year-old apprentice chef. It's so much fun to make and doesn't take long to prepare. However, it requires some concentration in the mixing of the ingredients. You can use this mixture to make choux puffs or Paris Brest.

60 g (2 oz) unsalted butter
¼ teaspoon salt
125 g (4 oz) plain (all-purpose) flour, sifted
4 large eggs
1 egg yolk mixed with 1 tablespoon cold water, for glazing

Preheat the oven to 205°C (405°F). Line a baking tray with baking paper.

Combine 250 ml (8½ fl oz/1 cup) water, the butter and salt in a saucepan. Bring to the boil, reduce the heat and add the flour, stirring vigorously with a wooden spoon until it forms a smooth sticky mass. Remove from the heat and set aside to cool for 3–4 minutes.

Mix in the eggs one at a time, stirring with a wooden spoon. Spoon the mixture into a piping bag fitted with a 1 cm (½ in) plain nozzle.

To make small choux puffs, pipe small mounds of pastry 2 cm (¾ in) in diameter and 2 cm (¾ in) apart on the prepared tray. To make large choux puffs, pipe mounds of pastry 6 cm (2½ in) in diameter and 2 cm (¾ in) apart on the prepared tray. To make Paris Brest, pipe a ring 1 cm (½ in) thick and 5 cm (2 in) in diameter onto the tray.

Gently and lightly tap the top of each choux puff or Paris Brest with a fork dipped in the egg yolk and water mixture.

Bake for 20 minutes, then reduce the temperature to 150°C (300°F) and cook for a further 20 minutes. Turn off the oven and leave the choux pastry to dry in the oven for about 1 hour. Cool on a wire rack before storing for up to 3 days.

Puff Pastry

MAKES 1.15 KG (2½ LB)

Puff pastry is a wonderful pastry and a great favourite of mine. It's outstanding in tarts, vanilla slices and biscuits.

500 g (1 lb 2 oz) plain (all-purpose) flour
1 teaspoon salt
400 g (14 oz) unsalted butter

1. Blend together the flour, salt and 125 g (4 oz) of the butter. Slowly add 250 ml (9 fl oz/1 cup) cold water and blend until well incorporated. Form the pastry into a ball, wrap it in plastic wrap and refrigerate for 30 minutes. Cut the remaining butter into narrow slices, about 1 cm (½ in) thick.

2. Remove the pastry from the refrigerator and roll it out on a lightly floured surface to a square about 1 cm (½ in) thick. Lay the butter in the centre of the pastry and fold the four edges into the centre to completely envelop the butter.

3. Roll out the pastry to a rectangular strip 1 cm (½ in) thick. Take the bottom end of the strip and fold it up one-third of the way towards the top. Now fold the top down over the first fold to form a neat rectangle with no overlapping sides.

4. Turn the pastry around a quarter turn to the right. Repeat the above process and make a small impression with your fingertip in the top right-hand corner of the pastry. Wrap the pastry in plastic wrap and refrigerate for 20 minutes.

5. Remove the pastry from the refrigerator and position it so that the finger mark is in the bottom right-hand corner. Now repeat steps 3 and 4 twice.

The pastry may be used immediately or kept in the fridge for a few days. If you wish to keep it longer, wrap it in plastic wrap and store it in the freezer.

Sponge Finger Biscuits

MAKES 20

These are the biscuits of my youth. They can be served with fruit, ice cream, mousse or custard. They need to be prepared with a delicate hand and, once in the oven, avoid opening the door, especially in the first 12 minutes of cooking.

4 large eggs, separated
115 g (4 oz/½ cup) caster (superfine) sugar
4 egg yolks
80 g (3 oz) plain (all-purpose) flour, sifted
50 g (2 oz) icing (confectioners') sugar, for dusting

Preheat the oven to 220°C (430°F). Line a baking tray with baking paper.

Using electric beaters, beat the egg whites on high speed. When they begin to stiffen, add 50 g (2 oz) of the sugar and beat until stiff peaks form.

Place the 8 egg yolks and remaining sugar in a bowl and use electric beaters to beat until pale and creamy. Gradually fold the egg-yolk mixture into the egg whites, then fold in the sifted flour.

Spoon the mixture into a piping bag fitted with a 1.5 cm (½ in) round nozzle. Pipe the biscuits in 8–10 cm (3–4 in) lengths on the prepared tray. Sprinkle the top with icing sugar and bake for 15–18 minutes. If they start to brown too much, reduce the oven temperature.

Allow to cool. The biscuits will keep for three to four days in an airtight container, but are best eaten fresh.

Meringue

MAKES 20

Meringues are very popular and fun to make. They're scrumptious with ice creams and sorbets or with a simple dollop of whipped cream.

3 large egg whites
pinch of cream of tartar
115 g (4 oz/½ cup) caster (superfine) sugar
50 g (2 oz) pure icing (confectioners')
    sugar, sifted

Preheat the oven to 150°C (300°F).

Using an electric mixer, beat the egg whites and cream of tartar until the whites stiffen. Gradually beat in half the sugar until the whites are shiny and becoming firmer, then beat in the icing sugar and remaining sugar.

Line two baking trays with baking paper, using a little of the meringue mixture to stick the paper to the trays. Spoon the meringue mixture into a large piping bag fitted with a 1 cm (½ in) nozzle and pipe finger-shaped meringues 6–8 cm (2½–3 in) long onto the prepared tray.

Bake for 20 minutes, then reduce the temperature to 100°C (210°F) and cook for 1 hour. Turn off the oven and allow the meringues to dry in the oven for 2–3 hours before storing them in an airtight container for up to one week.

Hazelnut Praline

MAKES 200 G (7 OZ)

These fabulous caramelised hazelnuts are delicious served with ice cream or sprinkled on fruity desserts.

55 g (2 oz/¼ cup) caster (superfine) sugar
2 drops red wine vinegar
150 g (5 oz) roasted skinned hazelnuts

Lightly oil a sheet of baking paper and place on a baking tray.

Combine the sugar, vinegar and 2½ tablespoons water in a small saucepan. Bring to a simmer over medium heat and cook until the sugar starts to caramelise. Make sure it doesn't burn.

Add the hazelnuts and, using a wooden spoon, stir over low heat for 2 minutes or until the hazelnuts are well coated with the caramel.

Very carefully transfer the caramelised hazelnuts onto the oiled baking paper and spread the nuts using a wooden spoon (don't touch the mixture as it will be very hot). Set aside to cool completely, then store in an airtight container until required. You can break it into pieces for easier storage if you wish.

Make the praline by cutting the caramelised hazelnuts into small pieces using a large knife or blender.

Crème Pâtissière

MAKES 625 ML (21 FL OZ/2½ CUPS)

This pastry custard is used in tarts, is delicious with fruit and is often used to make soufflés. You can make it lighter by adding a little whipped cream to the cold custard.

500 ml (17 fl oz/2 cups) milk
½ vanilla pod, split lengthwise
4 egg yolks
100 g (3½ oz) caster (superfine) sugar
50 g (2 oz/⅓ cup) plain (all-purpose) flour, sifted

Combine the milk and vanilla pod in a saucepan and bring to the boil. Remove from the heat and whisk well so the vanilla seeds flavour the milk.

Whisk the egg yolks and sugar in a heatproof bowl for 2 minutes. Whisk in the sifted flour.

Remove the vanilla pod from the milk. Pour the hot milk onto the egg-yolk mixture, whisking well.

Return the mixture to the saucepan and bring to the boil over medium heat, whisking constantly. When the mixture is just boiling and has thickened, transfer to a heatproof bowl. Whisk for a few seconds more, then set aside to cool before storing in the refrigerator for up to four days.

Crème Anglaise

MAKES 750 ML (25 FL OZ/3 CUPS)

This runny egg custard is so lovely. I use it as a sauce for cakes and it goes well with both fruit and chocolate. It's also a great ice cream base.

5 egg yolks
145 g (5 oz/$2/3$ cup) caster (superfine) sugar
500 ml (17 fl oz/2 cups) milk
$1/2$ vanilla pod, split lengthwise

Using electric beaters, beat the egg yolks and sugar in a large heatproof bowl until the mixture forms a ribbon. This will take about 5–8 minutes.

Combine the milk and vanilla pod in a saucepan and bring to the boil. Pour the hot milk onto the egg mixture, whisking well.

Return the mixture to the saucepan and, using a wooden spatula, stir over medium heat until the custard thickens slightly and lightly coats the back of the spatula. Do not allow the custard to boil.

Remove from the heat, strain the custard into a heatproof bowl and whisk for a few seconds more. Set aside to cool, then refrigerate until required for up to four days.

Cocoa Sauce

MAKES 220 ML (7½ FL OZ)

This flavoursome sauce can be prepared in minutes for a special treat served with poached fruits, ice cream or a piece of cake. You can reduce the sugar if you find the sauce too sweet.

30 g (1 oz/$1/4$ cup) dark Dutch (unsweetened) cocoa powder
1 tablespoon sugar
$2½$ tablespoons cream

Combine 100 ml ($3½$ fl oz) water with the cocoa and sugar in a saucepan. Bring to the boil, stirring well to dissolve the cocoa. Stir in the cream and simmer for 15 seconds.

Strain the sauce into a bowl and set aside to cool before storing it in the refrigerator.

Chocolate Ganache

MAKES 300 ML (10 FL OZ)

A ganache is a beautiful silky chocolate sauce. It works perfectly as a cake topping and is delicious served with ice cream.

300 ml (10 fl oz) cream
300 g (10½ oz/2 cups) dark cooking chocolate, cut into small pieces

Bring the cream to the boil in a saucepan. Remove from the heat and stir in the chocolate until melted and smooth. Set aside to cool before using.

Lemon Butter

MAKES 300 G (10½ OZ/1½ CUPS)

For this recipe you will need a stainless-steel bowl that fits into a saucepan, creating a double boiler.

juice of 1 large lemon
2 teaspoons finely grated lemon zest
95 g (3 oz) caster (superfine) sugar
3 large egg yolks
100 g (3½ oz) unsalted butter, cubed

Bring a saucepan of water to the boil, then reduce the heat to low and place a stainless-steel bowl over the saucepan.

Add the lemon juice, lemon zest and sugar to the bowl, then whisk in the egg yolks and butter. Continue whisking until the mixture thickens and becomes smooth. When the mixture is thick and creamy, transfer it to a cold bowl and whisk for a few seconds. Set aside to cool before refrigerating for up to one week.

Apricot Sauce

MAKES 450 ML (15 FL OZ)

Use perfectly ripe apricots to make this tangy sauce. Serve it with ice cream or a slice of sponge cake or other plain cake.

6 ripe apricots, halved and stoned
juice of $\frac{1}{2}$ lemon
juice of 2 oranges
$\frac{1}{2}$ vanilla pod, split lengthwise
2 tablespoons sugar

Combine all of the ingredients in a saucepan. Bring to a simmer and cook for 10 minutes or until the apricots are soft.

Discard the vanilla pod. Using tongs, remove as much of the apricot skin as you can. In a food processor, blend the mixture to a purée. Set aside to cool, then refrigerate until required.

Raspberry and Vanilla Sauce

MAKES 300 ML (10 FL OZ)

This wonderful sauce can be served with cakes, ice cream and fruity desserts.

juice of 1 orange
juice of 1 lemon
80 g (3 oz/$\frac{1}{3}$ cup) sugar
$\frac{1}{2}$ vanilla pod, split lengthwise
300 g ($10\frac{1}{2}$ oz) fresh or frozen raspberries

Combine all of the ingredients in a saucepan. Bring to a simmer, then cook for 5 minutes.

In a food processor, blend the sauce to a purée, then strain into a bowl. Set aside to cool. Refrigerate until about 10 minutes before serving.

Blackcurrant Coulis

MAKES 300 ML (10 FL OZ)

Blackcurrant, *cassis*, is a very popular berry in France. It has a powerful, intense flavour. In Australia, blackcurrants are mostly sold frozen.

juice of 1 orange
juice of 1 lemon
80 g (3 oz/⅓ cup) caster (superfine) sugar
½ vanilla pod, split lengthwise
300 g (10½ oz) fresh or frozen blackcurrants

Combine all of the ingredients in a saucepan. Bring to a simmer, then cook for 5 minutes.

Push the fruit through a fine strainer, then set aside to cool. Refrigerate until 10 minutes before serving.

Mango and Passionfruit Coulis

MAKES 300 ML (10 FL OZ)

This lovely fruit sauce is perfect with vanilla and fruit ice creams and as an accompaniment to berries and stone fruits. You can omit the passionfruit if you prefer just a mango coulis.

1 large mango
juice of ½ orange
juice of 1 lemon
1 tablespoon sugar
pulp of 2 passionfruit

Peel the mango and cut the flesh into pieces. In a food processor, blend the mango flesh, orange juice, lemon juice and sugar to a purée. If the mango is a little fibrous, strain the sauce into a bowl.

Stir in the passionfruit pulp. Refrigerate the coulis until required. If it is too thick, add a little orange juice before serving. If the mango is not quite ripe, you may also wish to add a little extra sugar.

Blueberry and Raspberry Coulis

MAKES 300 ML (10 FL OZ)

The availability of blueberries has increased in the last few years. As with grapes, much of the flavour and colour comes from the skin rather than the pulp. This coulis is beautiful with fruit desserts. You can serve it in small glasses or a sauceboat, or spoon it onto plates around a slice of cake.

65 g (2½ oz) blueberries
100 g (3½ oz) raspberries
seeds of ½ vanilla pod
juice of 1 orange
juice of ½ lemon
2 tablespoons caster (superfine) sugar

In a food processor, blend the blueberries and raspberries with the vanilla seeds, orange juice, lemon juice and sugar.

Strain through a sieve, discarding the berry seeds. Refrigerate the coulis until required.

Raspberry Coulis

MAKES 300 ML (10 FL OZ)

Raspberries make a delicious coulis that is both refreshing and extremely versatile.

300 g (10½ oz) raspberries
juice of 1 orange
juice of 1 lemon
2 tablespoons caster (superfine) sugar

In a food processor, blend all of the ingredients to a purée. Strain the coulis to remove the seeds, then refrigerate until 10 minutes before required.

index

A

almonds
almond and blueberry galette 15
apricot and almond cake 50
caramelised apricots in almond
custard 152
floating islands 76
orange and almond cake 11
pear and almond tart 64
pithiviers 23
Plombières ice cream cake 141
poached apricots and peaches
with toasted almonds 121
sweet pastry with almonds 177
apples
apple cake 36
apple and Calvados pie 56
apple and quince terrine with
raspberry and vanilla sauce
117
English-style apple pie 65
French apple tartlets 58
rhubarb and apple crumble 161
tarte Tatin 68
apricots
apricot and almond cake 50
apricot and hazelnut dacquoise
10
apricot sauce 187
apricot tart 61
caramelised apricots in almond
custard 152
frozen apricot soufflé with
hazelnut praline 146
poached apricots and peaches
with toasted almonds 121
stewed cherries with strawberries
and apricots 104

B

baking tips 5

bananas
banana loaf 18
flamed bananas with rum 157
kiwi, banana and strawberry
gratin 168
berries
blood orange mousse 94
caramelised red plums with
berries 116
lemon and berry pavlova rollover
35
mixed berries with Kirsch in tulip
baskets 110
summer pudding 100
see also blueberries; raspberries;
strawberries
biscuits, sponge finger 181
Black Forest roulade 12
blackcurrants
blackcurrant coulis 188
mandarin mousse with
blackcurrant coulis 84
blood orange, mango and pineapple
salad 120
blood orange mousse 94
blueberries
almond and blueberry galette 15
blueberry and raspberry coulis
189
peaches with raspberry coulis
105
stewed blueberries with crème
chiboust 112
butter cake 22

C

cakes
almond and blueberry galette 15
apple cake 36
apricot and almond cake 50
banana loaf 18
Black Forest roulade 12

butter cake 22
carrot and hazelnut cake 47
chestnut and chocolate cake with
raspberries 42
chocolate sponge 12
Christmas ice cream cake 133
confit fruit cake 27
flourless chocolate cake with
a chocolate and hazelnut
topping 30
hazelnut meringue cake with
chocolate ganache 46
lemon and coconut semolina cake
with pistachios 26
my most popular chocolate cake
34
orange and almond cake 11
orange and passionfruit cupcakes
38
pithiviers 23
Plombières ice cream cake 141
poppyseed cake 39
prune and Galliano cake 24
rum savarin with tropical fruits 44
Savoy sponge 51
soft-centred chocolate cakes 43
strawberry sponge cake 20
caramel 76
caramel Paris Brest with chocolate
hazelnut cream 31
caramelised apricots in almond
custard 152
caramelised red plums with
berries 116
crème brûlée 86
crème caramel 80
hazelnut praline 184
carrot and hazelnut cake 47
charlotte, chocolate, with raspberries
77
cheese
baked lemon cheesecake 8

Acknowledgements

I am most grateful to my wife, Angie, who assisted me in almost every aspect of this project. Heartfelt thanks to my brother, André, and sister-in-law, Joëlle, who gave me great experience in their Parisian boulangerie-pâtisserie during my younger years. I am indebted to all the great chefs and pastry cooks I have worked with over forty years for sharing their knowledge with me.

A big thank you to everyone at Hardie Grant, especially Paul McNally, Lucy Heaver and Heather Menzies, photographer Mark Roper, food stylist Simon Bajada and home economist Caroline Jones, who assisted me in preparing the beautiful cakes and desserts in the photographs.

And merci to all the readers with a sweet tooth, and to my dentist!

Cup conversion table

This book uses metric cup measurements: 250 ml = 1 cup. In the US a cup is just under 8 fl oz, and American cooks should be generous in their cup measurements; in the UK a cup is 10 fl oz and British cooks should be scant with their cup measurements.

1 teaspoon = 5 ml and 1 tablespoon = 20 ml.

This edition published in 2012
First published in 2012

An SBS book

Published in 2012 by Hardie Grant Books

Hardie Grant Books (Australia)
Ground Floor, Building 1
658 Church Street
Richmond, Victoria 3121
www.hardiegrant.com.au

Hardie Grant Books (UK)
Dudley House, North Suite
34–35 Southampton Street
London WC2E 7HF
www.hardiegrant.co.uk

Cataloguing-in-Publication data is available from the National Library of Australia.
100 Best Cakes & Desserts
ISBN 9781742703862

Hardie Grant would like to thank The Works, Bed, Bath and Table, Mud Ceramics, Step Back Antiques and Izzi and Popo for some of the props used in this book.

Publishing Director: Paul McNally
Project Editor: Lucy Heaver
Editor: Justine Harding
Design Manager: Heather Menzies
Concept Designer: Gayna Murphy
Photographer: Mark Roper
Stylist: Simon Bajada
Production: Penny Sanderson

Colour reproduction by Splitting Image Colour Studio
Printed and bound in China by 1010 Printing International Limited